MW01032503

Glendale Public Libraries
5959 West Brown St.
Glendale, AZ 85302

THE ORDEAL
OF
OLIVE OATMAN
A True Story of the American West

THE ORDEAL
OF
OLIVE OATMAN
A True Story of the American West

Margaret Rau

MORGAN
REYNOLDS
Incorporated

Greensboro

THE ORDEAL OF OLIVE OATMAN *A True Story of the American West*

Copyright © 1997 by Margaret Rau

All rights reserved.
This book, or parts thereof, may not be reproduced in any form except
by written consent of the publisher. For information write:
Morgan Reynolds, Inc., 620 S. Elm St., Suite 384
Greensboro, North Carolina 27406 USA

Photos courtesy of the Arizona Historical Society

Library of Congress Cataloging-in-Publication Data
Rau, Margaret.
  The ordeal of Olive Oatman : a true story of the American West / Margaret Rau. —
1st ed.
  Includes bibliographical references and index.
  ISBN 1-883846-21-8
      1. Oatman, Olive Ann, 2. Oatman, Mary Ann, d. 1852—Captivity. 3. Indian
captivities—Southwest, New. 4. Apache Indians. 5. Mohave Indians I. Title
E99. A6R25 1997
979'. 004972—dc21

                                                    97-28182
                                                    CIP

Printed in the United States of America
First Edition

Dedicated to my littlest new friends,
Sophia and Joseph Riley

Contents

Olive Oatman

Chapter One

The Journey Begins

Olive Oatman had never experienced anything like the few days she spent in Independence, Missouri. The muddy streets of the rowdy river town were lined with buildings—stores, saloons, rundown hotels. Here and there stood huge Conestoga wagons used by the traders who needed to carry quantities of goods, but were too heavy for the settlers to get across streams and up hills. The thoroughfares teemed with a noisy assortment of the strangest people that Olive, fresh from quiet farm country on the Illinois prairie, had ever seen. Rakish gamblers, sailors on leave from their boats drawn up at the river wharf, merchants looking out of place in fashionable broadcloth suits and shiny top hats, mountain men in buckskins and boots, their eyes gimlet sharp from staring into long distances, filled the dusty streets. All these people were shouting, laughing, yelling. Now and then a sudden burst of gunfire made Olive jump.

Olive was traveling with her family in a caravan organized by Jim Brewster, who wanted to establish a colony on the lower Colorado River on land ceded to the United States after the Mexican War. The travelers planned to leave west from Independence and journey on the Santa Fe Trail, a set of parallel ruts cut by the wheels of the Conestoga wagons.

The Oatman family, along with some of their neighbors, decided to set-out on the trip despite their knowledge that the often harsh treatment by American soldiers had created a rising fury toward the white invaders on the part of the Commanches, Pawnees, Arapahoes, and others. It was not easy to decide to risk one's life on such a dangerous trek. But when Royce Oatman announced the Oatman family would embark on the trip, no one was more excited than twelve-year-old Olive.

Royce and his wife thought the hot, dry climate of the Southwest would help to relieve his severe back pain and would help with six-year-old Mary Ann's persistent cough. Mrs. Oatman, also named Mary Ann, was afraid that her favorite child suffered from the dreaded tuberculosis. The Oatmans also thought the wider horizons would give their children greater opportunities. In addition to Olive and Mary Ann there were six other children in the family: Lily, sixteen; Lorenzo, fourteen; little Royce, eight; Carrie, three; and two baby brothers.

Other families from the Oatmans' tightknit, devout community decided to join the Brewster party, including their best friends, the Wilders and the Kellys. They would not have to make the journey with complete strangers, and would have fellow worshippers at the nightly prayer vigils.

Royce sold the family farm for $1,500, enough to carry them through the trip. The farm wagon was repaired. It would serve as their covered wagon. Old worn spokes were replaced and the wooden rims covered with iron plating to protect them on the rough road. Curved staves were fitted into slots and canvas was spread over them. Then all the farm implements, guns and ammunition were loaded. Space was limited and the children had to leave most of their favorite things behind.

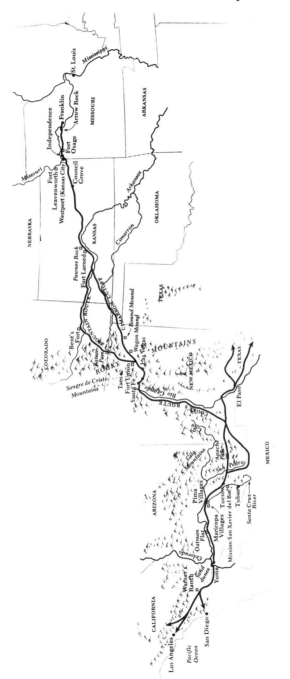

The Oatman family followed these trails on its journey to the Arizona desert.

The work went on for days, but finally the farm animals deemed strong enough to make the journey were gathered and the mules were hitched. As the preparations drew to a close, Olive's excitement at beginning the journey was replaced by a deep sadness at what she was leaving behind. But Olive loved her father and trusted his judgement. He kept his promises. If he assured her they were going to a better place, where life would be easier, she believed him. She shook off her sadness, and foreboding, and walked as cheerfully as possible beside the wagon on the first leg of the journey. They planned to meet up with Jim Brewster and the other travelers in Independence.

Olive did not have long to spend in the fascinating river port. On August 9, 1850, Brewster gathered the group together and led them out of Independence. The party consisted of fifty people, men, women and children—and twenty wagons.

Everyone brought along extra teams of oxen as well as cows, horses, and watchdogs to bark a warning should Commanches attempt to steal upon the camp at night.

At the first camp just outside Independence, Brewster called a meeting to lay out a few ground rules. Then the caravan was ready to move. The wagons went first. The cattle, horses and dogs followed, herded along by the single men and boys, including Lorenzo riding horseback.

Mrs. Oatman, like many of the wives, sat on the high wagon seat holding the baby on her lap and the reins of the oxen team in her hands. Mr. Oatman walked beside the team, driving it on with smart cracks of the whip.

The two younger children sat beside their mother. The others would rotate rest times in the wagon There was one exception— Mary Ann. Her mother insisted she take longer rest periods than the others. Olive seldom took her turn. She enjoyed walking because the oxen were so slow it was like a leisurely stroll through open prairie country.

For a week the caravan traveled west, going no more than fifteen miles a day. Every time the caravan stopped at a campsite there was a great hustle. The men would unharness the cattle and put them out to graze. Then they would arrange the wagons in a circle to provide protection from attack. This was common practice among travelers. Inside the circle, the men would start setting up tents for the night. Meanwhile, the children would collect kindling for cooking fires, and the women would begin preparing the evening meal, chatting among themselves as they worked.

As twilight deepened to night, the tiny fires seemed to Olive like mere sparks in the great lonely prairie that stretched away on all sides. Out in that loneliness, moving farther and farther away from the safe little farm house, Olive would sometimes hear the melancholy baying of gray wolves. Then she would crowd closer to the last embers of the dying fire, thinking of the four comforting walls that had once sheltered her.

Perhaps it was the loneliness and loss that was affecting the adults as well. As the days progressed, Olive heard the grownups arguing. Some arguments almost ended in fights. Most were about religious differences. Sometimes the arguments became so fierce that some members threatened to quit the caravan and return home. Brewster managed to persuade them to continue to Council Grove where things could be worked out.

About 150 miles from Independence, the travelers finally reached the little trading post of Council Grove. It wasn't much of a post. Located in tribal territory, it stood on the fringe of a thick stand of trees—oak, hickory, walnut, butternut. A stream, dappled with the shadows of overhanging leaves, sparkled among the trees.

The travelers stayed a week. During those days, Lily spent much of the day in camp helping her mother with the great mountain of washing that had to be done. All the women at camp were doing their washing too. Soon, all the covered wagons were festooned with all kinds and sizes of clothing flapping like flags in every breeze.

Olive had the chore of watching over her brother, Royce and little sister, Mary Ann. Mary Ann was no problem, always staying close to Olive's side, but Royce was a tease, mischievous and full of fun. Olive often had to chase him over the rolling prairie. She kept a close lookout when he decided to dabble his feet in the little stream. It would be just like him to tumble head first into it if she didn't grab him first. But whatever he did, she could never be angry with him. His laughter, great infectious gales of it, made up for everything. Olive had to laugh with him, Mary Ann joining in with her clear, sweet child's voice.

The men were busy too. Lorenzo and his father joined the others as they felled some oak and hickory trees. Then they lopped off the branches and hewed the trunks into rough lengths of timber that they lashed to the bottoms of the covered wagons. The wood would come in handy to make new axles if the old ones should break. The men had heard that beyond Council Grove it was impossible to find hard wood of any kind. The cottonwood trees were too soft for their purposes.

Brewster, meanwhile, was making use of the week at Council Grove to select leaders from the group. He met with them in private to iron out differences and lay down more rules. Chief of these rules was that Sunday would be a day of rest, and for church services.

Another rule, a very important one, was that from then on a vigilant watch should be kept to protect against raids. Beyond this point Commanches, Pawnees, Arapahos, and Sioux were becoming more hostile. Infuriated by the invasion of their lands by the increasing numbers of whites and the presence of American soldiers, they were attacking careless caravans, stealing livestock, killing unwary travelers. Because the caravan would be especially vulnerable after dark, Brewster and his council worked out a series of two-hour watches that would last from dusk to dawn. Every able-bodied man stood guard duty at one of these watches.

By the time the caravan was ready to set out, Olive noticed that people seemed more closely bound together, ready to forget their petty quarrels.

Beyond Council Grove, the trail led through mile after mile of grass so tall that only the tops of the covered wagons could be seen. Because they looked so much like the sails of ships at sea they had been dubbed "prairie schooners."

The prairie schooners moved on through the prairie grass. Sometimes breezes rustled the drying grass. Olive kept wondering if the stealthy sounds were Pawnees quietly stealing upon them. Then she would strain to catch the sound of an eerie whistle, the Pawnee signal for attack. All the children caught the apprehensive mood and became less exuberant. Feeling trapped by the tall grass, they walked close beside the wagons.

The party slowed at the crossing of Cottonwood Creek. Here the wagons had to be unhitched and lowered by rope down the slippery bank. At stream level they had to be hauled through the water and up the opposite bank. Meanwhile, the women and children were removing shoes and stockings and fording the creek. The younger Oatmans were carried over by Lily and her mother. Olive, leading Royce and Mary Ann by hand, splashed happily with them through the water.

Finally, the men and boys drove the cattle and horses across the stream and up the bank to join the wagons. It was a time-consuming job and by the time the oxen were reharnessed to the wagons most of the day was gone.

Cottonwood Creek was only one of several streams that had to be crossed before, at last, the caravan reached the Arkansas River at a place called Great Bend, where the river turned northwest. A ten-mile deep band of sand dunes flanked the stream and the party traveled on the far side of the dunes. The tall grass had given way to a shorter variety called buffalo grass because it was the favorite grazing food of the buffalo.

Suddenly, it seemed the whole world lay open before Olive's eyes. Vast prairies rolled away to break against the distant mountains. Through the grasslands wandered the trails of bison. Here and there the caravan passed whole cities of little prairie dogs. Olive laughed to see the tiny brown sentinels standing at attention on their mounds, heads cocked, then all at once popping back into their holes. Free of the enclosing grass, all the children's spirits rose. They scampered over the short turf, turning brittle now with the approach of autumn. From under their feet, grasshoppers leapt away with a whirring rattle. Overhead, flocks of migrating birds were already winging south, their cries now loud, now faint, as they disappeared.

Just beyond the Great Bend the travelers met their first Commanches. It was Sunday morning following church services when several of them asked to visit the camp and were admitted, much to Lorenzo's dismay.

Olive, drawing Royce and Mary Ann close to her, had to agree with her brother about allowing the Commanches to visit. She wondered why no one seemed to remember the warnings they had been given back at Council Grove. She watched the Commanches wander at will around the camp, inspecting everything. It was only when they drew apart and began fitting arrows to bows that the travelers wakened to their danger. There was a scramble for weapons and the Commanches found themselves staring into the muzzles of guns.

Quickly lowering their bows, the Commanches shouted friendly farewells and took their departure. The crisis had passed but it had been a close call. It left behind an uneasiness that infected the whole party.

This feeling was heightened when the group reached towering Pawnee Rock, whose smooth sandstone surface was etched with the signatures of those who had passed this way. Perhaps the older Oatman children, along with others, stopped to carve their names here too.

Once the rock bore hundreds of names, but unfortunately the record is lost because the facing that contained them was sliced away in later years to provide building blocks. But whether Olive left her mark or not, surely she must have been troubled by the sight of the lonely graves that lay at the foot of the rock—graves of Americans, marked with crosses, and of Pawnees and Commanches—signs that there had been bloody clashes here in the past.

Beyond Pawnee Rock, the caravan continued to follow the Arkansas River. Once this land fed millions of bison. But the herds had been decimated since the trail opened. The Brewster caravan may have chanced upon a herd. But it is more likely that their game was grouse, rabbits and deer. With these they augmented their daily diet of beans, corn, rice and hardtack made from unleavened flour.

After some weeks the travelers reached the site of modern day Dodge City. Here the road divided into two branches. One led north through the mountainous country of Colorado. Going by the mountain branch usually took about seventy-two days. Traveling south by the Cimarron cutoff could save ten days travel. But that branch was dangerous, so dangerous the Mexicans called it *Journada de Muerto*—Journey of the Dead. In stark contrast to the lush prairie lands to the north, the Cimarron cutoff was a sixty-mile stretch of waterless desert lying between the Arkansas and Cimarron Rivers. European travelers coming this way called it the American Sahara. Nonetheless, because it was the shorter route, it was the unanimous choice of the Brewster party.

On the far side of the Arkansas they met a government caravan. The faces of the men were worn and pale. Their clothes were gray with dust. Olive listened as they described the dangers ahead. They warned the travelers to take along plenty of water and to portion it out carefully. People had died of thirst wandering over the desert in search of water.

Chapter Two

Journey of the Dead

As the government train went on its way, the emigrants set to work. Using sauce pans, bottles, pails, every utensil they had, they began scooping up water from the Arkansas River and storing it in their wagons. But the warning about Commanches made them all nervous. One man, going to the river, pail in hand, spied two little girls topping a rise nearby. With their aprons over their heads to shield them from the sun, they looked like Commanches wearing headdresses. "Injuns! Injuns! Injuns!" the man began yelling as he rushed back to camp. Tripping on a wagon tongue, he sprawled headlong. The pail flew from his hand with such a clatter that the dogs began barking furiously.

Tensions exploded in gales of laughter. Even as she laughed, Olive felt a little sorry for the embarrassed man who was stumbling awkwardly to his feet.

At last they had all the water they could carry and were ready to set out. But their passage across this Sahara turned out to be quite pleasant, as the heavens opened and spilled out rains in abundance. Pools everywhere slaked the cattle's thirst, though they still suffered hunger because forage was scarce.

Whenever the caravan camped for the night, the children, wild with excitement, were free to explore the strange new land they had entered. Olive kept her little brother and sister away from rattlesnakes, scorpions and tarantulas.

It was not easy to keep Royce out of trouble. He was easily enthralled by the creatures that scuttled across the desert. He could have easily strayed away and become lost.

While the children were exploring the desert, the adults were still watching for Commanches. None appeared, though there were several false alarms, such as the day two hunters in search of game flushed out some antelope. Seeing the antelope headed in their direction, a flock of children ran to a nearby ridge. There they began jumping up and down, waving their arms wildly to drive the antelope back toward the hunters. The hunters began running in the opposite direction. The shocked children stared after the fleeing men. Then they rushed to camp to see if anyone could explain the men's strange behavior. No one could until the hunters burst into camp, their eyes glazed with horror.

"Injuns!" they yelled. "Injuns doin' a war dance on a ridge back there."

"You brave men," the campers jeered. "You got guns in your hands and scuttle away from children just trying to help you."

Olive laughed with the others. The hunters had behaved in such a silly way.

For many days people joked about the hunters. Finally the caravan reached the Cimarron. It had been almost two months since they left the Arkansas. On the other side of the Cimarron, they found themselves in sheep country. Olive could make out small flocks watched over by Mexican herdsmen.

About five hundred miles from Big Bend the travelers came upon the town of Mora, in what is now New Mexico. After the vast emptiness through which the caravan had been passing,

Olive welcomed the sight of the adobe houses, the homes of three hundred people who came out to greet the newcomers.

Black haired, black-eyed children, their brown cheeks ruddy from the sun, gathered around the Oatman family and began asking questions in their unfamiliar tongue. Olive wished she knew what they were saying. She wanted to see inside their homes. Small, they still looked comfortable and safe to Olive.

The adults, with the help of an interpreter, carried out their transactions. The town earned most of its living selling supplies to passing caravans. The travelers bought quantities of fresh mutton and for the next few days enjoyed mutton stew.

There was disquieting news from the Mexicans, who told them that the Colorado River area was in Apache country, and the Apaches were on the warpath. They were attacking both Mexican and American intruders. When they attacked, it was often a massacre. This gave the travelers pause. The terrain was becoming more difficult. The land was mostly desert, broken here and there by flat-topped mesas.

In this rugged country of glowing red landscapes, the vibrant colors of the earth below matched the brilliant blue sky that domed it. Though it was now autumn, the light that poured from the sun and radiated off the rocks and earth was still so penetrating that it hurt the eyes. Despite the shade hats the children wore, their eyes became swollen and red. The heat pressed upon them from the sky and earth alike, dampening even Royce's high spirits. Dragging their feet, the children stumbled along, always keeping a half-hearted lookout for dangerous snakes, whose harsh warning rattle could spell death for the unwary.

The grownups were also growing tired of the long, tedious

journey through this arid land so foreign to them after the green country east of the Mississippi River. The enthusiasm that had stirred them at the beginning of the journey was wilting under the hot sun. At night they tried to ignore the constant yapping of coyotes, now sounding distant and melancholy, now nearby and strident.

By day the shadowy wings of vultures circling greedily overhead haunted them. And as if to impress them further, bones of fallen oxen were strewn along the way, bleached skulls staring back at them from eyeless sockets. There was always the nagging fear of Apaches waiting on the route ahead.

Olive began to notice that among the grownups tempers were becoming shorter. Quarrels were starting to break out again. Finally matters reached a climax at the Santa Fe Pass, near a place called The Forks, where the trail divided into two branches. One, the Cooke-Kearny route, led south and would eventually end in southern California. The other branch led to the Mexican city of Santa Fe.

Jim Brewster announced that he planned to stop here. Anyone who wished to stay with him was welcome to do so. Thirty people with twelve wagons agreed to join him. The others, including the Oatman family, decided to press on. They were no longer thinking of stopping on the Colorado River. Instead, they would go on to California, well out of Apache territory. This decision meant that they would have to pass through the very heart of the Apache homeland. It was with some misgivings that they parted with their companions and set off for the little Mexican town of Socorro that lay on their route.

Chapter Three

Apache Country

It was late autumn, and the Mexicans of Socorro were reluctant to part with supplies. They stayed a week in the town, trying to scrounge up enough for themselves and their livestock. What they could purchase was expensive. Money was dwindling away. Poorly supplied, they set out again. Their new goal was the Rio Grande River that flows south through eastern New Mexico. They could find good forage there.

The water was so scarce it had to be rationed. Sometimes the thirsty children would catch glimpses of lakes shimmering in the distance. Olive knew they were mirages. But the little ones kept crying to go to the inviting water.

The oxen also suffered. There had been so little forage along the way they could scarcely plod along and needed frequent stops. Added to the Oatmans' problems was the sense that the Apaches were always lurking. Shortly before the caravan reached the Rio Grande, two of their finest horses were stolen.

The party spent a week along the Rio Grande before pushing on. The way now led over mountains. The oxen had to be pulled up the steep ascents and held back on the down slopes. It was a job that required strength and skill. Royce Oatman accepted the challenge with his usual energy and optimism.

One day they came to a place so bleak that they were filled with utter despair. Before the sun set, a freezing gale had risen that lasted through the night. When Olive wakened the next morning, snow blanketed the distant mountains. Yet here, where they needed it so much, no rain had fallen.

The freezing wind continued to howl. The younger children whimpered, and the older ones stood shivering in their winter woolens. No one had had water the previous day and night. Throats were parched and burning. Tongues were swollen.

The men began to search for the cattle that had scattered in their search for forage and water. As the men began the roundup, one of them saw a dark green ribbon that descended the slope of the distant ranges. Trees! It had to be trees! That meant water!

Forgetting weariness, nagging thirst, and bone-chilling wind, the men gathered in the cattle and harnessed the oxen. Again the caravan set off, this time for the distant hills. It took most of the day to reach the trees, where the efforts of the caravaners were rewarded. With shouts of relief they found themselves in a pleasant meadowland broken by copses of thickly set trees. Through the meadow flowed a sparkling stream, its banks lined by the trees the men had seen in the distance.

The waters were ice cold, too cold to drink, but that was quickly remedied because wood was plentiful. The children, their spirits restored, raced here and there gathering kindling. Soon a fire was briskly burning and everyone had a warm refreshing drink. Best of all, the men discovered the stream was alive with fish. It was also a magnet for the wildlife that lived here—turkeys, antelope, wild sheep.

The group stayed a week in this pleasant place. The livestock grew fat on the rich pasturage. Then one day Olive saw three fierce-looking Apaches approach the camp. The Apaches expressed their friendship with gestures and smiles. But Olive noticed how the unwelcome visitors were eyeing the horses, the oxen and the supplies spread out on the ground. Finally, the caravaners got their guns and, brandishing them at the Apaches, drove them off. After they had gone, the camp remained apprehensive.

That night Olive slept only in short snatches and she knew by their tossing and turning that the others were restless too. The dogs were filling the night with a continual clamor—barking, snarling, growling, snapping. Olive knew it meant the Apaches were still nearby. She was relieved to know that her father and the other men were out there with muskets primed for an attack. Hour after hour went by and nothing happened.

It was not until the next morning that Olive found out what had really occurred. In the darkness the Apaches had overrun the camp. Their tracks were everywhere. They were gone now but they had taken twenty head of cattle and horses with them.

Olive watched as the men left to recover the stolen cattle. Soon the search party returned, empty-handed. They had to give up after the hoof prints descended into deep canyons where the men dared not follow.

Now the group was so short of animals they had to leave some wagons, luggage, and food behind and crowd what they could into three wagons. The Oatmans still had their wagon but only one team of oxen, two cows and one horse. They could no longer spell the animals no matter how worn out they became. Worse still, they had lost the protection provided when the wagons were placed in a defensive circle. The little party would be especially vulnerable to an attack by the Apaches.

The route now led through a greener countryside. As the travelers went forward, they began passing little settlements inhabited by Mexicans. They could offer little in the way of supplies because the Apaches had ravaged their fields.

More than fields had suffered. They also came upon the ruins of villages, reminders of Apache attacks. Olive stared at the crumbling walls and roofless rooms. Had any of the people who lived there managed to escape, or were they all dead?

The road was growing rougher and rougher, the weather more uncertain. Sometimes it was sunny, other times dark and dreary. There were days of howling gales or pounding rains. Always, whether the days were sunny or bleak, the nights were freezing; and always there was the fear of the Apaches, unseen but lurking nearby.

Eighty or ninety miles along the route the party came to the larger town of Tucson standing in the midst of a farmland oasis. So far this town had escaped an Apache attack, but the unprotected fields had been razed, leaving inhabitants with little food.

Despite their lack of supplies, the Mexicans welcomed the visitors eagerly. Conversation between them was easy now because the travelers had been picking up Spanish along the way. Candidly, the Mexicans explained that the Apaches were more afraid of the guns and fighting skills of one *Americano* than they were of twenty Mexicans. That was why the people of Tucson wanted their visitors to stay with them, offering them good land for farming and good pastures for the few remaining cattle they had left.

The travelers lingered in Tucson a month trying to make up their minds what to do. During their stay, the Mexicans overwhelmed their visitors with hospitality. There was no need here for Olive to keep an eye out for Royce as he played with a host of friendly little boys. Girls with shiny black braids surrounded Olive and Mary Ann. They invited them into their homes where their mothers welcomed them as honored guests, pressing tidbits on them and inviting them to stay for family dinner.

At the end of the month most of the Americans decided to remain in this friendly place. The Oatman children must have longed to stay. Surely they were disappointed when their father decided to join the Wilders and the Kellys and push on. But they accepted his decision without complaint because that is what they had always done. After all, he was the one who would know what was best. Even their mother made no objection.

Again, Olive had to say farewell, this time to new friends. Then the three families set out, taking the remaining wagons with them. They were left with very little in the way of supplies.

In mid-February, and ninety miles out of Tucson, they arrived in the little village of Pimole, the home of the Pima peoples. The Pimas welcomed them warmly. They had been at war with the Apaches for some time, and had managed to drive off all attacks. Though their fields were destroyed and they had scarcely enough left for themselves, they told the visitors they were welcome to stop.

Again, discussions were held. Should they go or stay? The Wilders and Kellys decided to stay with the Pimas and grow enough grain for the last lap of their journey. If a larger, better-supplied caravan should come along, they could join it.

It took Royce Oatman a while to arrive at his decision. He made it only after weighing the alternatives. On the one hand, his family and the oxen were worn out. They could use the rest, and the Pimas by their numbers could provide protection. On the other hand, there was little to eat here and the Oatmans' store of food would not last very long.

Could a single family traveling alone through 150 miles of Apache country reach the safety of Fort Yuma without being attacked? It was during this period of indecision that two travelers, a Dr. Lecount and his Mexican guide, rode into Pimole. Dr. Lecount told Oatman that he and his companion had ridden to Fort Yuma and back again without encountering a single Apache. It was his opinion that the area was safe.

Oatman made his decision. He would continue on.

Pimole left behind, the forlorn little group slogged on. It was all they could do to keep the starving oxen moving. The trail led westerly over increasingly rugged terrain. The oxen were now so weak they could not pull the wagon up hills. Urging, whipping, pushing, hauling had no effect. Olive looked at the gaunt animals with pitying eyes. The pattern of their rib cages showed plainly beneath their sagging hides. Olive knew how the animals felt because she too felt drained and spiritless. All the same she wished the oxen would move because when they didn't all the children had to pitch in and help. Mrs. Oatman would start handing down the belongings. The children and their father would carry them up the hill. When the wagon became light enough, the oxen had to be goaded, hauled and pushed to the top where everything had to be reloaded.

Even when the trail was level, travel was sometimes difficult because rain had turned the trail into a quagmire where the wagon and the oxen would become stuck. It took the efforts of the whole family to push and pull them free.

Six days out of Pimole the Oatmans were overtaken by Dr. Lecount and his assistant who were heading back to Fort Yuma.

Dr. Lecount promised that when he got to the fort he would ask the commander to send out a rescue party. After separating from the Oatmans, Dr. Lecount rode another thirty miles where he stopped for the night.

In two days time the Oatmans reached Dr. Lecount's camp site. Unfortunately, they missed the warning Dr. Lecount had left for them written on a card that he had tacked to a tree. The warning advised the Oatmans that Lecount and his guide had encountered Apaches. They had driven them off but had lost their horses and had to travel to Fort Yuma on foot.

If the Oatmans had seen that warning they would have turned back to the safety of Pima territory. Instead, they continued. The year was circling into March. Spring in the desert brings warmer weather. The days were so hot at times that the cattle refused to move, and the Oatmans had to restrict their travel to dawn and dusk. Sometimes they even traveled after nightfall as a waxing moon gave them light.

Olive was becoming aware of a new and frightening fact. Her father, always so strong, so optimistic in the face of every danger, now seemed to shrink in upon himself. In his gray face, drained of blood, his sunken eyes seemed fixed upon a future too terrible to name. Sometimes Olive heard him speak to their mother of his foreboding as of a dark cloud he saw hovering over his family. Listening to him, Olive felt that cloud too, staining the whole glowing landscape with its ominous shadow.

Late in the afternoon on the 18th of March 1851, the family finally reached the bluffs overlooking the Gila River. Two hundred feet below, Olive could see the Gila rushing along, swollen by recent rains and melting snows from the mountains where it had its source. The trail led across the Gila and continued westward to Fort Yuma, located where the Gila joined the Colorado River.

It wasn't much trouble getting the oxen to go down hill, perhaps because they sensed the chance of finding green foliage below. At the foot of the bluff they entered deep shadow, though high above the long rays of the sun were still gilding the tops of the bluffs. Mr. Oatman started to lead the oxen across the river, which was now running so deep and strong that at times oxen and humans almost lost their footing.

Midstream they mired on a sandbar. All the family's efforts to break it loose failed. Dusk was coming on. They would have to spend the night here. The team was unyoked and all the animals were turned loose to wander along the river's edge to graze. Then with head bowed, shoulders stooped, Mr. Oatman set off in search of kindling. Olive watched the forlorn figure until it disappeared down a small tributary. What had happened to the once-vibrant father she had known and depended on? Fear touched her with its cold breath.

By the time her father came back with the kindling and built a fire the twilight turned chilly; a wind had begun to blow in blustering gusts through the canyon. Shivering, the children huddled around the fire while their mother prepared the meal— a bowl of cornmeal mush apiece. They ate crowded together, listening to the wind yammering like the voices of lost ghosts.

Afterwards, rolled up in their blankets, the children tried vainly to sleep. They chattered among themselves throughout the windy night. Their subject was the Apaches.

"If they come, I'll run. Fast as I can. I'll run," Mary Ann declared.

Nine-year-old Royce said, "I'll fight them, I will!"

Fifteen-year-old Lorenzo exclaimed, "I'll take my father's gun or a club and drive them off."

Olive spoke last, gravely, sadly, "One thing is certain," she said. "I'll not be taken captive. I'll fight them off as long as I can and if I lose I'll just kill myself."

Lily, the oldest, said nothing then. But later that night she whispered to Olive that she had heard their parents murmuring among themselves. Once she had heard their father starting to cry. He had sobbed for more than an hour while their mother whispered comforting words to him.

Father crying! Olive thought about their strong, optimistic father crying in the night. She had never heard him cry before. It was as though a dark and empty hole opened below her.

At last the sky began to lighten. Olive saw early morning sunlight glistening on the tops of the pine trees on the plateau above them. With the growing light the canyon did not look as desolate as it had the night before. The wind had died away, the river had fallen.

Lorenzo and his father set about gathering the oxen. They hitched them to the wagon, pulled it from the mire and hauled it to the far side. Yet the worst task lay ahead—to mount the steep bluff.

Again the cattle refused to budge. The children and their father had to carry their belongings to the plateau. Even with the wagon empty the oxen still would not budge, languid in the heat that now filled the ravine.

The Oatmans were forced to wait until late afternoon to try again. It was during this long wait that Olive first became aware of her mother's patient strength. It was she who calmed their fears and gave them courage, while their father sat on a great boulder beside the wagon, his face buried in his hands. Once close to tears, he suddenly exclaimed in a cracking voice, "Oh, mother, in God's name something terrible is going to happen to us. I feel it! I know it, mother! What have I done? What have I done?"

The family was finally able to get both team and wagon up the steep bluff to the plateau. By this time the sun was sinking. While in the east a pale moon nearing its full was rising above a distant mountain range. From this point on the family planned to do much of their traveling by night to avoid the growing heat. They would have to cover eighty miles in this way before they reached Fort Yuma.

Olive saw a jumble of broken land stretching away. Over all that expanse the only foliage she could discern was an occasional tree. Mr. Oatman brought kindling from the river and lit it. Mrs. Oatman busied herself with supper—bean soup.

Mr. Oatman ate alone, keeping his head averted as though he was ashamed. When he finished eating his food, he got to his feet with heavy movements and announced they should start packing and be on their way.

The children began preparing to leave. At this time Lorenzo happened to look down the steep bluff. On the trail below he saw a band of men dressed in wolf skins steadily climbing toward them. "Look, father, look!"

Mr. Oatman came over. Spasms shook his body. When he finally spoke he said in a calm, gentle voice. "Don't be afraid. They won't harm us."

Chapter Four

Yakoa! Yakoa! Yokoa!

The children stared round eyed as the band of men reached the top of the bluff. Mr. Oatman greeted the newcomers the way he had always greeted the native people he had met in Illinois. In a cordial voice he invited them to sit with him. Then, making use of the Spanish he had picked up, he told them that he wished to be friends.

The men responded in Spanish that they were Apaches who also wanted friendship. They asked for tobacco and a pipe so they could smoke the peace pipe to cement the friendship.

Olive watched as her father produced a pipe and tobacco and the men passed it around in silence. Olive was aware that though her father was doing his best to appear calm, underneath he was seething with tension. She wondered if the Apaches had noticed it too. They displayed a growing arrogance. She felt reassured when Lorenzo whispered that at least they didn't seem to have any weapons.

"If only Pa would put on a bold front," Lorenzo added. "Just get his gun, threaten them. Make them scared enough to go away."

His father continued to sit there meekly. When the Apaches asked for food, he patiently explained that the family had very little to share. Finally, after the Apaches continued to insist, he gave in and passed around some chunks of hard bread that the family had left from supper. The Apaches accepted it greedily, wolfing it down. When it was gone, they demanded more.

"I just wish Pa'd refuse them this time," Lorenzo muttered. Instead, their father grudgingly doled out another half portion of the precious bread. These conciliatory actions only seemed to make the Apaches more contemptuous. Olive saw how their eyes kept shifting over the family belongings, then the wagon, the oxen, the cows, and the single horse. They got to their feet and walked off a short distance where they squatted on the ground and began to hold a council among themselves.

By this time their behavior had become so threatening that Oatman was at last stirred to action. He told his wife and the children to start packing and to do it as quickly as possible. As they worked, they spoke softly among themselves about their fears. The Apaches paid little attention to them. Instead, they kept staring down the trail along which they had come. Were they checking to see if the Oatmans were just the first in a long train of covered wagons that would soon follow? If so, they would be ready to melt away.

Then suddenly the Apaches made up their minds. With an ear-splitting war cry, YAKOA! YAKOA! YAKOA! they pulled out clubs from underneath their wolf skins and brandished them in the air.

Lorenzo was the first to be struck across the top and back of his head. Olive watched in horror as he dropped to his knees. Another blow flattened him. The Apaches dragged his limp body to the brink of the bluff and left him.

One Apache pulled Olive aside. She thought he was going

to club her, but he merely held her tight. Olive watched the Apaches leave Lorenzo, now bleeding from ears and mouth, and batter little Carrie and her younger brother. Then they started raining blows on her father. Powerless to help, Olive had to watch her father struggling, bleeding, groaning under the swinging clubs until at last he sprawled silent to the ground.

Another Apache was battering Lily, dear sister Lily, to whom Olive had so often gone for comfort over some childish grief. Olive saw her sister crumple under the fierce blows. Nine-year-old Royce was standing on the outskirts staring in frozen silence. Olive wanted to shout to him to *Run, run*, though she knew it would be useless. An Apache was already striding toward him. The child let out one terrible haunting scream as the club fell on him. Olive watched as the small, once vibrant body dropped to the ground shuddering convulsively. Then with a soft moan the little boy died.

A heartrending cry made Olive turn her head to see her mother crouched against the wagon clutching her youngest child to her breast. Over her stood an Apache, club raised high. A single blow killed the little boy instantly. Then a rain of blows began to fall on his mother; her agonized moans roused Olive to action. She broke free of her captor to race to her mother's side. A strong hand hurled her back. Shivering uncontrollably, a wave of dizziness swept over her. Had she been struck too? It was her last thought as she plunged into darkness.

When Olive woke, she found herself lying on the ground. She struggled to her feet, bewildered, wondering where she was and why all her family were strewn motionless and bloody around the wagon. Then she looked down to see little Mary Ann standing beside her. The child was sobbing, whispering over and over, "Oh, Olive, mother and father and all our brothers and sisters, they're dead. The Apaches have killed them all. Only you and I are left."

Olive shuddered. Turning to the Apaches, she began to beg them in Spanish to kill her too. Her pleas only sent them into gales of crazy laughter and mocking jeers. Olive fell silent, her attention drawn again to the sobbing little girl beside her. She realized then she couldn't die, not as long as this frail child depended on her.

The Apaches had already begun plundering the possessions of the family. They worked methodically, stripping grownups and children of their boots, shoes and hats. Olive and Mary Ann were forced to give up theirs.

Other Apaches were using clubs and rocks to break open the boxes and chests containing clothing, food, tools, taking anything they thought might be of use to them. Emptying the wagon, they came upon the feather bed. Olive watched as her mother's precious mattress was carelessly ripped open. Seizing handfuls of the soft, white down, the Apaches tossed it into the evening breeze and stared open-mouthed as the light feathers floated away.

Next they removed the wheels of the wagon and tore off the canvas covering. They packed their loot in separate bundles among themselves. Finally they unyoked the oxen and freed the cows and the horse from their tethers. Then, driving the girls and livestock before them, they set off down the trail toward the Gila River.

Stumbling in the graying day, their bare feet soon cut and bruised on the rocks and stones, the girls clung to each other. Whispering together, they wondered what the Apaches had

This drawing of the Apache attack on the Oatman family was based upon Olive's memory of the event.

planned for them. Why had they been spared?

"Do they plan to kill us by torturing us to death?" Mary Ann asked, and Olive could only keep tight hold of her little sister's hand. It was all the protection she had to give.

At the foot of the bluff they had to wade the Gila again. Then for another half hour they rushed along a faint trail that meandered through a dark corridor between beetling cliffs. Finally, the narrow chasm opened to form a small clearing. Ashes from an old bonfire showed that this place was often used as a campsite.

The Apaches stopped here to rest, removing their packs. They began collecting armfuls of kindling. Bringing out some flint stones and wads of wild cotton, they soon had a fire going. They unpacked some beans from the Oatmans' supply and put them on to boil in a clay pot. They took some flour and mixed it with water, forming a dough that they flattened and cooked in the ashes. When the meal was ready, one of them offered some to the girls. He taunted and insulted them as he offered them the food, and they turned away, refusing to touch it.

The Apaches ate greedily, for this spartan diet was a feast to them. After they finished, they rested an hour. Olive and Mary Ann crouched before the warming fire. Olive, her arm around Mary Ann, remembered how she had boasted she would never be taken captive and, if she were, she would kill herself. How innocent and childish those remarks had been, so far removed from reality. There was nothing here with which she could have killed herself even if she tried. There were always Apaches watching for any suspicious move she might make in that direction, and there was still little Mary Ann to think of, Mary Ann so close and dear beside her.

The section of the desolate Arizona desert where the attack occurred is now known as Oatman Flats.

While they waited, the moon rose above the tiers of mountains to the east. Olive thought she had never seen a more beautiful moonrise. The largest undimmed stars gleamed like diamonds.

The moonlight showed Olive that they had not traveled very far from the place where her family had been massacred. On one bluff the skeleton ribs of the stripped wagon rose black against the silver light. With an aching heart, Olive thought of her shattered family lying deserted up there, in death, neglected and alone. She wept silently, yearning to return to visit them one more time, if not to bury them, at least to say goodbye.

The Apaches waited until the moon rose high enough to shed its light on the deep ravine. After an hour or so they were ready to move on. The cattle were quickly rounded up and placed in the care of several Apaches who immediately went off with them. The rest shouldered their packs and with the girls set out in a different direction.

The trail they followed meandered between high peaks and tiers of rocky buttresses. They moved at a fast pace, and when the girls fell behind they were beaten or threatened with clubs and the war cry *Yakoa*!

The trail became steeper and the girls stumbled along over beds of sharp rocks. After a few miles, Mary Ann sank to the ground, unable to go on. The Apaches first yelled at her, then began to beat her. But she remained indifferent, even when they threatened to kill her. Olive began pleading for her sister's life. Finally, one Apache threw his pack to the others. He picked up Mary Ann and tossed her over his shoulder, carrying her limp body as though it were a sack of grain.

Olive, near fainting as well, forced herself to walk beside the

Apache, keeping close watch over Mary Ann. Her moaning had stopped but Olive saw her eyes opening and closing, opening and closing, as if she were trying to wake herself. Olive spoke to her softly but got no answer. Mary Ann sank into a sleep so deep that Olive wondered if she were dying.

At midnight the Apaches halted for a few minutes. After that they did not stop again until the next noon when they reached an expanse of sandy soil enclosed by towering mountains. Here and there great oaks spread their welcome shade. The Apache who had been carrying Mary Ann dropped her to the ground beside Olive. Apparently, the ride on his shoulder had revived the child.

Both girls rested while the Apaches sat around waiting. After about two hours the men who had driven off the livestock arrived, bringing two of the oxen and the horse with them. The other animals had been killed, dressed and then hung up to dry, to be retrieved later.

The Apaches now slaughtered the oxen and the horse, skinned and dressed them, and sliced the meat into small slabs. These were packed in tight bundles and distributed among the Apaches to be added to the packs they were already carrying.

This work completed, the men gathered kindling and started another fire over which they grilled some flesh. This with bits of burnt dough bread and a little bean soup made up the noonday meal. The girls were each given a small piece of stringy beef along with some burnt bread and soup. This time hunger made them accept the food.

Two hours later the Apaches were ready to resume their march. They tried to force Mary Ann to walk again, but she could scarcely stand. They beat her but she didn't even cry out.

At last an Apache flung her over his shoulder and they started.

By this time Olive was scarcely able to walk herself. The long tramp over stretches of sharp rock and boulders had badly lacerated her feet. The Apaches brought out pieces of tough animal hide and, putting Mary Ann down, they tied the scraps to both girls' feet and shoved them forward, stumbling and lurching.

Around ten o'clock that night the Apaches stopped again, this time in a dark ravine. The girls were told to lie down on a patch of sand and sleep. They lay side by side covered by two blankets thrown over them—blankets they recognized as ones their family had owned. For a long time sleep would not come. Staring up at the shining stars, they softly pointed out to each other those constellations their father had shown them. Arms around each other, they wept, overwhelmed by homesickness.

Early the next morning the girls ate another meal of dough and beans and a small scrap of meat, and the trek started again. This day the Apaches moved at a greater speed than ever before, though the road was rougher than any they had traveled. When the girls couldn't keep up they were pushed and hauled along, their bodies battered and bruised. It was only later that they learned the Apaches wanted to get out of this area as quickly as possible because white travelers often used this route.

They met no one that day, but the next day around noon a band of hostile Indians ambushed them by suddenly dashing from behind a rock pile brandishing bows and arrows. They shouted to one another and pointed at Olive. Then one of them fitted an arrow to his bow and shot at her. Luckily the arrow, its tip smeared with a deadly poison, only pierced her full skirts.

Another Indian was about to take a shot when Olive and Mary

Ann were dragged back by their captors. Two of them then stood in front of the girls, shielding them while demanding to know the cause for this hostility. Shaking his fists and shouting insults, the Indian who had shot the arrow explained that he had lost a brother to the hated white man and wanted revenge. Finally, the angry Indians left and the Apaches continued their trek.

On the fourth day after the massacre the girls at last came in sight of a cluster of thatched huts. They were bone-tired, every part of their bodies ached and their feet burned with pain.

Stumbling along, they saw as they drew nearer a swarm of men, women and children rushing out of the village to greet them. Some men were naked; others wrapped only in blankets or animal skins. Most of the women wore short skirts made of bark. Evidently, the news of the successful raid had already reached them, for as they approached they began singing a wild victory chant.

Soon the raucous crowd had surrounded the girls. They began pushing them forward to an open space in front of the huts near a huge pile of brush and bark. The men hoisted them onto the pile. After that long, cruel hike through the wilderness, were they now to be tortured and burned alive?

Men, women and children were forming a circle around the brush heap. Others carried stones they beat with their clubs to make a wooden tattoo of sound. Others blew horns in rhythm while fiddlers played a squeaky accompaniment on crude fiddles made of bark, across which they drew their bows.

To this wild orchestra of sound, the chanting and dancing began. Round and round the dancers went, leaping into the air, circling the girls on the brush heap. They pranced with mincing steps until in front of the girls each dancer would stop and make wild gestures while stamping the ground furiously. Finally, with a frightful yell, the dancer would bend nearly to the ground before dancing on to give the next person a chance.

The smallest children were the worst. Their wild taunts, jeers, pinches, painful jabs and pokes sent the adults into gales of frenzied laughter.

In every wild taunt the girls could sense the hatred the Apaches felt toward the whites who were taking over their lands. Would their hatred end with another massacre here? Dizzy, their heads pounding, the girls could only hope that their deaths would be swift and as merciful as the poisoned dart on the arrow would have been.

In the end the dancers exhausted their rage and slipped away. The captors took the girls down from the brush pile. They were told mockingly that from then on they would be the slaves—*onatas* in the Apache language—of the entire village. With these sneering words they were turned over, weak and shaking with fear, to the women of the chief's household, their new supervisors.

Chapter Five

The Onatas

The girls received no better treatment from the Apache women than they had from the men. The women, who were brutally treated by their husbands, now took out their seething anger on the helpless girls. They stripped them of their long dresses and gave them short skirts like their own, laughing derisively when the girls blushed over their scanty attire.

Early the next morning Olive and Mary Ann were handed baskets and sharpened sticks. Under a blazing sun, the women drove their slaves into a rocky country with a few desert bushes and stunted mesquite trees. Boulders heaped on boulders formed grotesque silhouettes against the sky. The girls' job was to hunt for edible roots and dig them up.

At first the women had to show them the signs that told them where the roots could be found. Then with their sharpened sticks they had to break through the ground. At first they had little success, though they tried so hard that they wore blisters on their hands.

Whenever the girls failed to find enough roots they were beaten. In the evening, when they returned from foraging, they met the men, who had spent the days on the banks of a nearby stream or lying about on the rocky ledges that surrounded the village. The men snatched the few roots the girls had managed to collect and then beat them mercilessly because they had gathered so few.

Though they were tired, aching and hungry, the girls had no food or rest. Instead, the women continued to heap chores on them. Most of the chores were unnecessary. The women just wanted to prove their power over the helpless white slaves. If the girls didn't move quickly enough, they were beaten. Even the children were encouraged to make impossible demands of the slaves.

As Olive became more aware of the women's place among the Apaches, she began to understand the reasons for their anger. They, like the slaves, worked like beasts. They were denied the meat the men brought back from their occasional hunting trips. Instead, the flesh of the animals was boiled in a clay pot until it became mush, which provided the base for soup. The older women might be given a little of it. But the young women received none unless they were on the verge of starvation. Olive noted the frequent deaths of little girls and was sure it was the result of malnutrition. Even those who managed to survive grew into stunted, dwarfish adults, so in contrast to the well-nourished, muscular men.

Olive and Mary Ann, who were getting much less to eat than the Apache women, were becoming gaunt and weak. Mary Ann suffered the most. Finally, when she was unable even to creep along, the women supervisors ordered rest for her. When she had regained some strength, she was sent out again, but without any change in her meager diet.

As time went by, the girls were finally able to solve their problem. Now that they had learned how to dig up roots, the women relaxed their guard. The girls wandered off by themselves in their search. This meant they could eat their fill away from prying eyes. It might mean coming back with so few they would get a beating, but that was still better than starving to death.

The girls treasured this time alone for more than the extra food they could eat. It also gave them a chance to talk to each other freely. They even welcomed the arduous task of fetching wood and water because it kept them out for a whole day. Often during these times Mary Ann would come to Olive sobbing, "Oh Olive, I've tried so hard to please them. But it doesn't do any good. How long will we have to stay here, Olive? Let's try to escape."

Escape—that was on the minds of both girls. Sometimes they would spend hours laying their plans. Then Olive would notice how Mary Ann's eyes would sparkle.

"I can find a way out, I know I can," the child would cry eagerly. "And I can go the whole distance, Olive, as quick as they."

Olive remembered how Mary Ann had to be carried much of the distance to this place. She was sure that even if they could find the way back, Mary Ann would not survive the whole trip. Still, she could not find the heart to discourage her earnest sister. There were times after some especially cruel treatment that Olive herself was ready to consider escape. The two girls would then set the date, the hour, and the route they would take. But when the time came, they always lost their nerve.

Then one day Mary Ann approached her sister with a new idea.

"I know what we can do," the little girl exclaimed. "We can

pray to God to help us just as our mother taught us to do back home. If He won't deliver us, we can at least get Him to give us the grace to bear it all."

After this, the girls took every opportunity to pray together. Buoyed by the prayers, Mary Ann no longer complained to her sister or wept in the presence of her captors. She cheerfully did all the foolish tasks given her. Her mild, patient spirit seemed to touch the women. They began to relax their harsh treatment of both girls. Even the children started showing their affection, won over by the girls' gentleness so unlike the harsh manner of their parents.

By now the girls were beginning to understand the Apache tongue and learned something about their captors. They were, they said, no longer part of the main tribe, but were known as the Tonto Apaches—the Unruly Apaches. That was because they had tired of taking orders from the elders and had run away to live in this mountain wilderness. They were not, they bragged, as wicked as the main Apache tribe, adding that the girls should be grateful they hadn't fallen into those cruel hands.

The Tonto Apaches were developing their own traditions. Once a week a meeting would be held, attended by the whole village. At these meetings an elderly chief would give a long talk about the active years of his youth. The girls could make no sense out of the rambling recital, but the Apaches paid rapt attention.

The Apaches were also finding another source of entertainment—their *onatas* now that they could speak the language. Crowds would gather around the girls to fire question after question at them.

"How old are you?"

This photo of Apache warriors was taken several years after the attack on the Oatman family.

"How many white people are there in the world?"

"How wide is the big ocean?"

When the girls answered that there were two oceans, the Apaches wanted to know if whites owned lands that lay beyond that eastern ocean.

When the girls told them how many whites lived on this side of the ocean, some of the Apaches became angry and threatened to beat them for lying. Instead of beating them, the Apaches wanted to know how the whites could provide food for so many people.

Olive tried to tell them they could till the land and plant wheat or corn and other vegetables. The stream provided plenty of water. They would have enough food without foraging. At this the Apaches again lost their tempers, crying that they were not farmers and would never harm their mother earth by cutting into it. So Olive stopped talking about farm matters and instead reached back into her school days to recall the things she had learned there.

She told the Apaches that the stars above might be the home of whole worlds where other people lived. This time the crowd exploded.

"Lies! Lies! Lies!" they roared. "If people really lived up there they would all drop out."

Olive went on to explain that the world spun on its axis, once every twenty-four hours, and traveled around the sun once a year. It was this, she explained, that caused day and night and the four seasons.

"Lies! Lies! Lies!" the Apaches cried. "You're just like all Americans, all liars. Your parents must have taught you well from the time you were babies to make you such great liars."

Then they told the girls of their own philosophy of the white people. They were such liars, they said. Why were they so bad? It was because they were ruled by an evil spirit. It was he who had made them great and powerful. In the end he would destroy them.

Having put down the girls, they would go back to their questions, laughing and joking among themselves at the strange answers the girls gave. When the Apaches were at their ease like this, the girls saw a different side to their personality. They could be full of fun, some of it raucous but none of it malicious. Olive realized that to the Apaches they had become unique play things. It was very important to their safety that they keep the Apaches amused.

Not all the Apaches treated the girls' remarks with levity. The younger ones, and especially the women, came to them in secret to ask them for more details about the kind of life the white people led. Did the men have more than one wife? How did the white man treat his wife? If they farmed as Olive said they did, did the men help the women do the work? Were the women allowed to eat anything they pleased—meat for instance—or were they treated in the same way the Apache women were?

Olive answered all their questions earnestly. The one thing both girls learned early was never to express a wish to return to their own people. They quickly found that this so insulted their audience that it would result in a severe beating and a load of extra work to do.

Chapter Six

The Ki-e-chook

The only tribe the Tonto Apaches had any contact with were the Mohaves, who lived along the banks of the Colorado River, three hundred miles to the northwest. They were farmers and once a year they would bring their vegetables and grain to barter for skins and fur.

Late in the autumn of 1851 a large delegation of Mohaves arrived to trade. After they departed, rumors began spreading that they wanted to buy the slaves. But nothing seemed to come of it.

Then one day, as 1852 moved into March, Mary Ann came to Olive with some disquieting news. She had overheard a chief telling others in his hut that the Mohaves would be back soon to trade for the slaves.

"If the Apaches sell us, we'll have to walk more than three hundred miles to reach their village," Mary Ann wept. "I don't think I could make it alive, Olive. My cough is getting worse and worse."

Olive looked pityingly at Mary Ann's pinched face, seeing the glitter of fever in her flashing black eyes, now sunk deep in their sockets. She decided to join her sister at last in an attempt to escape.

Before they could set a plan in motion, an Apache chief came to tell them that a Mohave delegation had arrived and was interested in buying them. The daughter of the Mohave chief, Chief Espaniola, would make the final decision. But first, she wanted to talk to the girls. The Apache chief had come to bring them to her.

Olive was surprised at her first close look at the chief's daughter. She was still in her teens, probably no more than seventeen. And she was beautiful. Speaking in Apache, she told the girls that her name was Topeka. Then looking at them with pitying eyes, she began to ask a few questions. Their answers seemed to satisfy her because immediately after this interview she approved the contract.

But the trade still wasn't final. Many Apaches were ready to let the *onatas* go. Others objected loudly. Those who were most opposed were the ones who had slain the Oatman family and taken the girls captive. They shouted that they would rather kill them than let the Mohaves have them.

The argument lasted all night, while the sleepless girls waited to learn their fate. By sunrise everything was settled—they would leave with the Mohaves. The Apaches gave each girl a small piece of meat and a few roots and turned them over to Topeka. Their purchase price had been two horses, a few vegetables, a few pounds of bright beads, and three blankets.

Though everything was decided, some Apaches were still furious. They tried to get others to join them so they could rush the Mohave men and slaughter the slaves on the spot. Because no one would join them, they had to be content with screaming insults at the girls as they were led away. Other Apaches laughed derisively. But some children began to cry forlornly, putting out their arms to the girls and begging them to stay.

With the racket swelling around them, Topeka and the girls joined the three Mohave men who were waiting impatiently astride their horses. They all set off at a fast jog. Olive was surprised that Topeka, although the daughter of a chief, had no horse. She would accompany the slaves on foot, carrying a roll of blankets.

The first day the girls managed to keep up with the men. But by noon of the second they were too crippled to do more than hobble along. Olive begged the Mohaves to let them rest their sore feet, but the men responded with loud grumbling, even brandishing their clubs threateningly.

Topeka silenced the men with a word. Then she brought out pieces of hide from the bundle she was carrying and deftly bound them to the girls' feet. In a quiet voice she set each day's stint at no more than thirty-five miles. The men grumbled among themselves, but they didn't dare openly oppose Topeka's firm order. Though she might be on foot, she was still the daughter of the great chief.

Throughout the long, dreary trek that led over a jumbled, rocky terrain, Topeka walked with the girls. When each day's trek was completed, she helped them grub for roots for themselves and for the men. At night when the cold desert air settled over the land, Topeka stretched out on the ground with the girls, sharing her blankets with them.

On the late afternoon of the eleventh day, the girls climbed a last ascent and looked down into a narrow green valley watered by a sparkling river that wound in a zigzag course southward. The banks were lined by great cottonwood trees. Copses of these trees dotted the valley. Over everything towered the guardian mountains; their craggy peaks, rounded domes, and slender spires broke the skyline with their fantastic shapes. Clustered around the base of the mountains, green foothills rolled down to the valley floor.

Mary Ann's eyes brightened and she cried out in delight, all her weariness forgotten. "Here, Olive! Here is the place where they live! Isn't it a beautiful valley? It seems to me I should like to live here!"

"Perhaps you would rather stay here than ever go home," Olive teased. Topeka, looking down at the little girl's shining face, smiled her own delight at being home at last.

The party started to descend the trail into the valley. They began passing Mohave villages. As they went by, the villagers would rush out to greet them, shouting and dancing and singing to welcome Topeka, the beloved daughter of the chief. Hordes of children skipped along beside Olive and Mary Ann, laughing, shouting, and howling as they stared into the strange white faces.

Finally, the procession reached the bluff on which the chief's house stood, overlooking the river below. As they mounted the bluff, the whole household of the chief came out to welcome Topeka. Chief Espaniola himself was there, standing tall among the others. He was a well-built, muscular man, but what most impressed the girls was his kind expression that softened with affection as he greeted his daughter.

Beside the chief stood his gentle wife, Aespaneo. She also greeted Topeka joyously, then turned to smile at the girls. Olive noticed that several other women were smiling at them too.

Beyond the crowd stood the house itself, concealed behind cottonwood trees that stood so close together their branches interlocked. They formed an enclosure one hundred feet square.

Topeka ushered the girls past the cottonwood trees to a stout fence made of upright logs, each about six inches in diameter and twenty feet high. This fence enclosed a fifty-foot square. The girls went through the entrance in the fence to find themselves on a grassy lawn, so welcome to their torn feet.

Facing the lawn, more upright logs enclosed a twenty-foot square area. These logs formed the walls of the chief's house. A row of higher logs divided the interior of the house into equal parts and held up the roof—tree branches bound with an adhesive coating of dried adobe. The pounded earth floor of the large room had a few blankets spread over it. A small cooking fire smoldered by the open doorway.

When Topeka ushered her guests into this airy room, she dropped to her knees before the fire. A cake roasted in the ashes. She snatched it out and divided it into three parts, giving the larger part to Olive and sharing the rest with Mary Ann. They ate greedily, relishing the plain cake. It seemed to them they had never tasted anything so delicious.

Afterwards, Topeka told them they were to be part of a giant celebration that was to take place that night to welcome both her and the slaves. As darkness fell upon the valley, the people began gathering in the outer square. There were children of all ages, tall muscular men, and plump women. Olive and Mary Ann noticed how different the women appeared contrasted with the half-starved Apache women.

Kindling from the trees, dry brush, and leaves were heaped in the square and set alight. The girls were led to a prominent place well lighted by the bonfire, and the celebration began. Men, women, and even the littlest children danced and leapt high in the air, chanting their welcome to Topeka and proclaiming their pride at having acquired two white slaves.

As the hours went by, the children began falling asleep on the ground. The adults kept up their wild celebration until close to daybreak. Finally the merriment subsided. Parents began gathering up their sleeping children. The crowds started to disperse.

Topeka led the girls into the chief's house and showed them where to sleep. They lay side by side, covering themselves with the thin blanket Topeka handed them. Sleep would not come. There were so many unanswered questions to trouble them. They lay awake whispering to each other in worried voices.

Why had they been purchased and brought here? Was it to remove them farther than ever from white settlements? Was there, perhaps, a more horrible reason—torture, sacrifice, death in some terrible rite?

Finally worn out, the girls drifted off to sleep, but it was a sleep tormented by terrifying dreams. The nightmares woke them repeatedly as the hours went by. They were glad when dawn finally broke, filling the room with light.

Early that morning Topeka eased the girls' fears. She told them she had begged her father to buy them. She could not bear to see how the Apaches treated them. Though they were still slaves and would have to work for everyone, they would sleep in the chief's house and would have his protection.

For a few days following their arrival, the girls were allowed to rest and regain their strength. Those days were pleasant ones. From the bluff on which the chief's house stood, they could look down the valley that followed the course of the river for some thirty or forty miles.

No spot could be lovelier than this valley with its sparkling river that Jim Brewster had sung so sweetly of. Young wheat carpeted it, the green tide surging into silver under every passing breeze. In the warm sunlight, blackbirds were calling out among themselves. It was their mating season.

After several days of rest, the girls had light chores to do, mostly fetching water or gathering wood. It took them off the bluffs to the fields below, where with her farmer's eye Olive could see the methods the Mohaves used. Instead of plowing the land and sowing the wheat, the women had fashioned rows of little earthen mounds, placing about twenty seeds of wheat in each. Such a laborious and wasteful method, Olive thought.

Now the women were out in the fields again, stooping and rising, stooping and rising, as they planted their vegetable seeds—corn, beans, squash—between the mounds of wheat. As the girls passed by, the women would pause in their work to stare sullenly. Then they would spit out epithets. Though the girls could not understand the Mohave tongue, they did not mistake the meaning of these words. The women were cursing them.

Everywhere in the valley the girls were treated with the same mistrust and hatred. Only the chief's influence stood between them and death. But he could not shelter them from the hard work expected of them as slaves. Once the spring planting was finished, the girls' restful period ended. They joined the women on their foraging trips. They worked as hard digging for roots as they had in the Apache camp, and were treated almost as badly. They worked constantly and suffered whippings or scanty portions of food. Again they had to obey the commands of the children, who liked to see the slaves punished for not finishing all of their chores.

Then something happened that enhanced the value of the

slaves in the eyes of the Mohaves. The girls had taken to singing while doing their chores. Sometimes the songs were hymns they had sung at church or learned in school. Singing brought back happy memories that seemed to make the work go easier.

One afternoon, when Olive and Mary Ann were singing near the chief's house, they were overheard by a subchief and his family who were visiting Espaniola. Caught by the sound of the girls' voices, the subchief wanted to know who was making that strange, beautiful music. Espaniola sent for the girls and introduced them. The subchief and his family asked questions.

"What are you singing?"

"Where did you learn to sing like that?"

"Are all the whites such good singers?"

Finally, the girls were asked to sing for the family. They sang song after song until it was time for the subchief to take his leave. The girls' singing had so impressed him that during the days that followed he talked about it to everyone.

Eventually, visitors were coming from all over the valley asking for performances by the singing white slaves. Sometimes the girls sang for two to three hours. Afterward, the visitors gave them a small gift, usually a short string of bright beads or a piece of red flannel, the Mohaves' most cherished possession. After the girls had gotten several of these small scraps, they raveled the edges and tied them together to make a shawl.

As spring turned into summer, the girls had a new chore—gathering pods of the mesquite trees and hanging them in the huts to dry. Then the seeds inside were pounded into a kind of flour that made a sour mush. This mush was the Mohaves main diet after the vegetables ran out.

Accompanied by the women, Olive and Mary Ann went on

expeditions into the wilderness beyond the pleasant valley. It meant climbing rocky slopes, sliding into deep ravines, anywhere the mesquite trees grew. The girls were expected to fill their baskets. This was hard to do that year because for some reason the pods were scarce. Although they worked from dawn to dusk, they often had to return with their baskets only half full. That meant a whipping or being deprived of food.

Worse than the backbreaking work was the growing hostility of the Mohaves. It seemed to have increased since the girls had become popular as singers. No matter how hard they tried, they could not seem to please their captors. At first they could not understand why the Mohaves continued to feel such hatred for them. As they began to pick up the language, they found out why the Mohaves were angry. They thought the girls were planning to run away. Whenever Olive and Mary Ann talked to each other in English, the Mohaves would demand to know what they were saying. Whatever answer the girls gave, the Mohaves would shake their heads in disbelief.

"Don't lie!" they would shout. "We know what you're doing. You're plotting your escape. Have you made a good plot yet?"

The girls were bewildered by the questions. Escape? How could they escape? Surely they were now too deep in Indian territory to dream of that. What they did not yet know was that they were almost as close to Fort Yuma as they had been when living with the Apaches.

The Mohaves' grueling questions always ended with a vicious warning. "If you try to escape, we'll capture you, even if we have to follow you right to the white man's camp. We'll bring you back and you will suffer a terrible punishment."

One day the girls were resting in the hut after a hard day of foraging when Espaniola, along with several elders and two shamans, entered the house and approached the girls. Aespaneo, his wife, was summoned to explain their purpose. Aespaneo did her best. But the girls could not understand what she meant when she said the shamans had come to give them a *ki-e-chook*. Using gestures, Aespaneo made her meaning plain—the shamans were there to tattoo them.

Olive and Mary Ann had seen tattoos on some Mohave girls and had hoped this would never happen to them. They began pleading with the delegation to spare them. Their pleas were cut short by an elder.

"We know why you don't want our *ki-e-chook*," he told them. "It's because you plan to return to the whites one day. And you don't want to be ashamed when they see you marked as slaves."

Another added, "Every slave of ours is given this *ki-e-chook*. It will help us locate you wherever you may run. If we do not find you, other tribes seeing the *ki-e-chook* will know you belong to us, and they will return you no matter where you go."

Finally, the girls had to submit to the shamans, who began laying out their tools and ingredients—two sharpened sticks and two dishes. One contained the sticky juice of a weed they had gathered from the banks of the river. The other dish held black powder made by burning a blue stone that was to be found in the shallows of the river. The stone when burnt turned black, making it easy to pulverize.

With their sharpened sticks, the physicians pricked parallel rows of dots on the girls' chins, going deep enough to cause the punctures to bleed freely. Then they dipped their pointed sticks first in the sticky juice and then in the black powder. With the points of their sticks they pushed the fine powder into the puncture marks they had made.

It was a painful operation and it hurt even more during the two or three days of healing. The girls' first anguish over the tattoos began to fade with time. There were, they discovered, benefits from the disfiguring *ki-e-chook.* It seemed to convince the Mohaves that the girls would now have to give up all ideas of escape. As suspicions lessened, the others became more lenient toward the girls. They began plying them with questions about the way the white people lived. They were as curious as the Apaches had been before them.

The women were especially interested in finding out if the whites farmed. When Olive told them she and Mary Ann belonged to a farming family, they wanted to know how their family had planted their wheat. Olive told them about plowing the land to loosen the soil.

"If we had this beautiful valley," she boasted, "we could raise much more grain than you do just by plowing it first."

When the women wanted to know what a plow was, Olive made a crude model from sticks and showed how the plow loosened the soil.

At this point Olive might be interrupted by a cutting jibe from the men. "Whites are all mean and dishonest and can never be trusted." Then they would point out a huge domed mountain that dominated the valley. "The spirit of every white we kill is chained up there in a fire that burns forever," they bragged. "That place is the home of powerful evil spirits. If you try to go up there to rescue those spirits of your people, you too will be caught and chained along with them.

"On that mountain there is also a beautiful paradise," the

Mohaves continued. "Ruled by the great chief of all the Indians. Its hunting grounds are vast. And there are pleasures without number. Only the spirits of brave Indians are welcomed in that paradise. They must bring with them bows and arrows, clubs and knives, or they will lead a poor life."

The men would then go on to explain that among their people there were powerful shamans who could speak with the spirits and receive guidance on earthly matters. That was why the shamans were honored even by the highest chiefs.

"Do you whites have shamans, too?" the Mohaves would demand. "If so, they are guided by evil spirits to forsake nature and try to possess the whole earth as they do. But the spirits will lead you to destruction in the end and you will lose everything."

Having spoken, they would stalk away in triumph. Later, one of them might return and say, shaking his head wonderingly, "The whites are a singular people. I should like to know what you will be when many moons have gone by."

Chapter Seven

Famine

Autumn turned the wheat into a golden carpet that covered the valley. The women began their harvesting. They picked the ripened corn and gathered the squash and beans. From this bountiful store they saved out seed wheat and seed corn, squash and beans.

Now the feasting began. Olive, used to frugality, was distressed to see how greedily the Mohaves devoured the food, with no thought of the future. She realized there was not enough of it to last till the next fall. To satisfy the needs of the 1,200 people who lived in the valley, they would have to plant more acreage. She tried to tell them this but they only laughed at her. This was how things had always been done.

Feasting over, the women began planting next year's crop, laboriously stooping and rising as they carefully counted out and placed twenty wheat seeds in each moistened mound. The corn, squash, and beans would be planted in the following spring.

Autumn passed into winter and the Mohaves soon began to realize that the abundant rains of the year before were not going to repeat themselves this year. The hump of winter had passed with the Colorado still running low and sluggish. A light covering of snow blanketed the mountains. When it melted it would do little to replenish the river. The lake that last year had brimmed with water, providing fish to tide the people over, now was little more than a mud hole.

Food supplies were almost exhausted. Olive and Mary Ann had to join the women who went out each day to search for any mesquite pods they might have missed. Sometimes they worked under cloudy skies out of which poured dry, freezing winds. Numb with cold, their fingers swollen and half-frozen, the girls were scarcely able to pick the few dried pods they could find. When they returned to the village, the pods were snatched from them and they were beaten and given nothing to eat.

Spring brought only a few infrequent showers. The wheat was late sprouting and when the first sprouts did appear they looked pale and sickly. In the hard earth under the dry, cold air, they grew slowly in spindly sprays. Watching the wheat struggle for life sobered the Mohaves. Unless late rains came, a year of famine lay before them. Still hopeful, they planted their seed corn, squash, and beans.

The rains did not come. Out in the wilderness there were few blooms on the mesquite trees. That summer there were few pods to gather. Most of the time was spent grubbing for roots. The women had to travel farther and farther away to find any at all. Even then, there were never enough to go around. The women had to fight off the angry demands of the men to keep something for themselves. Often the two slaves had nothing at all to eat. Olive was looking gaunt and skeleton-thin. Mary Ann looked even worse. Sometimes the child could scarcely drag herself out to the wilderness to grub for roots.

"I can't live long unless I get something to eat," she would tell her sister. At other times she would upbraid Olive for not at least trying to escape. More often, she would dwell for hours on all the good food they had enjoyed at home. "Oh, Olive, if I could only get just one dish of bread and milk I would enjoy it so much."

By fall, after the harvest, the women's worst fears came true. After the seed needed for planting had been separated out, there was only enough left to provide the whole valley with a month's supply of food.

Weak and worn themselves, the women still followed their age-old custom. Again they prepared their mounds and planted their wheat. Olive noted ironically that this year they seemed to have learned their lesson, for they cleared and prepared more land than they ever had before.

One day, as the women were planting their wheat, Aespaneo came to the girls. She had been noticing how little they had to eat and decided to do something about it. Approaching her husband, she had persuaded him to allot the slaves some land of their own. He had finally granted them a thirty foot square of earth. Aespaneo took the girls to this plot marked out for them and told them it was theirs. She handed them seed wheat, seed corn, and squash, and told them that anything they grew on this land would be for their use alone.

That gift gave the girls fresh hope. They hid away the corn and melon seeds for spring. Then they began to prepare their little plot for the wheat. Feeling the earth crumble under their fingers awakened old memories of home. Back there they had done the planting in the spring when the bitter snows of winter were gone, the trees were putting out their leaves, and birds were nesting. They remembered how, barefooted, they had scampered down the sweet fresh furrows behind their father as he guided the plow. Sowing followed the plowing. Then would come the long, lazy summers as the wheat grew, a green sea across the prairie lands, turning to gold in the fall, promising a rich harvest.

This wheat they were planting now carried within it the same promise of future bounty. Early rains were already coming to the valley, foretelling the end to starvation if they could only hold out through the bleak winter. The supply of mesquite flour was fast dwindling away. It was getting harder and harder to find roots.

Starvation was abroad in all the villages. The Mohaves were growing ugly with hunger and fear. It was in this hopeless time that the rumor sprang up and quickly spread about a tree growing some sixty miles away that produced a berry called *oth-to-toa*. Several years ago this berry had kept people alive during another famine. The place where it grew was difficult to reach, for it lay in a craggy mountainous area.

Soon, people strong enough to make the journey gathered. Olive and Mary Ann were forced to shoulder their baskets and join the group. They set out. Mary Ann had gone only a short distance when she became too weak to continue. The others angrily ordered her on, threatening to beat her if she refused. Olive pleaded with them to let Mary Ann return to the chief's house, pointing out that she would only be a hindrance to them if she went. Finally, they gave in and let the little girl turn back.

Olive was grateful for that when she realized how rough the trail was. It took three days of arduous hiking to reach the stand of trees. The only food the party had to sustain themselves during the trek was the scanty supply of mesquite mush they had brought along.

Finally, they arrived at the place where the trees grew. The berry was much like the seeds of the mesquite bush, but it tasted better. Its juice, mixed with water, had an orange flavor. Olive's spirits rose. Here was food that could revive her sister. The long trek had not been useless after all.

Unfortunately, there were very few trees here, so six of the group, including Olive, set out to find a thicker stand. They traveled some twenty miles away from the camp until a large grove of trees, thickly covered with berries, rewarded their search.

Quickly, they filled their baskets and set off for the camp. By this time it was dark and they lost their way. Wandering about, almost dying of thirst, they stuffed themselves with the juicy *oth-to-toa* berries.

The berries, eaten in such quantity on empty stomachs, made most of them ill. Before noon of the next day, three of them were dead. Weak as the others were, they never thought of neglecting their ancient funeral customs. They struggled to gather the kindling and brush for a huge pyre on which they laid the bodies. Olive was sick and faint, wondering if she would soon be joining them on the pyre. Only the memory of Mary Ann kept her going.

Grieving for their dead comrades, the Mohaves shouldered their baskets and set out again, quickly finding the camp where the others were waiting. Traveling day and night, they finally reached the village. They had been away eleven days.

With a fearful heart, Olive hurried to the chief's house, afraid that Mary Ann was already gone. She found the child still alive but weaker than ever. During Olive's absence, she had eaten only scraps of food sneaked to her by Topeka and Aespaneo, out of sight of their starving relatives.

Looking at the wasted little form lying quietly in the shade of a cottonwood tree, Olive vowed she would never again spend the night away from Mary Ann. Perhaps it had been worth it, for Olive now had a good supply of the *oth-to-toa* berries, and she had learned a lesson. A starving person couldn't eat too many at once. She began to feed the little girl a small portion of soup made from the mashed berries. The child put on a little weight. She even appeared more alert.

If these berries could tide Mary Ann over the month or more that lay ahead, Olive thought, there would be hope for survival. Rain fell frequently on the valley. The Colorado had flooded in places, and when the heavy snows melted there would be more flooding. The lake, too, was beginning to fill again. It would be teeming with fish; blackbirds would nest and provide eggs. New plants would provide fresh roots. Mesquite trees would be blooming in profusion, promising plenty of seeds for the summer's gathering. When fall came they could harvest the crops from their own plot. The time of starvation would be over. Olive faced the days ahead with a lighter heart than she had felt for some time.

The sustaining power of the *oth-to-toa* berry proved to be temporary. Mary Ann began to weaken again. Olive was frantic. The little girl needed solid food, but where to find it? The pond still contained no fish. Most of the blackbirds had not yet arrived to build their nests. Olive spent much of her time searching for the nests of the few that had come early. When she found a nest, she would rob it of its eggs, carefully concealing them on her person. She knew that if she did not, they would be snatched from her, along with the few roots she could collect.

Whenever Olive produced eggs, Mary Ann's shining eyes

thanked her. The little girl ate them greedily, sucking them through the small hole Olive made in the shell. But the eggs were not enough. Day by day, the child's strength slipped away.

Mary Ann was not the only one who was suffering. Starvation was laying its dark hand upon the whole Mohave valley, turning Indian against Indian in frantic rages. The men assailed the women when they returned with their baskets, then fought each other for scraps of food.

Several children had already died. Others were dying. Adults were dying too, the weaker going first. Howls of grief filled the night and the day. The fires of the funeral pyres tainted the air with smoke and the odor of burning flesh.

The women had scoured the land for miles around in their search for roots. Olive knew that to find any now she would have to travel so far she might have to spend several nights away from Mary Ann. She feared for her sister's safety while she was gone.

Olive stayed close to the child, begging passersby for a little food. Sometimes the chief's wife or daughter would slip a morsel or so to them. Sometimes Olive would hear the loud voices of surly men who wanted to kill the little girl so Olive could be free to do her duties as a slave. Olive trembled then for the child's safety, knowing that only the chief's continued protection stood between her sister and instant death.

Mary Ann no longer seemed to worry about death. She thought only of her dead family.

"Dear Pa and Ma," she would whisper, "they suffered an awful death. But they are now safe and happy in a better and brighter land. And I shall soon be with them."

She spoke longingly of going to that land that she had learned about in church and from her mother. It was, she said, a land where there is no sorrow, where tears do not fall and all is beautiful. One day she told Olive, "I shall die soon. But you will escape." Then she began to sing. It was a hymn the family had sung together every twilight back in their home in Illinois.

The day is past and gone
The evening shades appear . . .

Olive tried to sing with her sister, but her voice broke and she could not go on. Mary Ann continued singing in her sweet childish voice. She sang song after song, day after day.

Forgetful of their own children dying back in the village, the astonished Mohaves began to gather around the little girl to listen to her singing. They stood for hours gazing into her calm, peaceful face. They had never seen anyone die this way before.

One day, Topeka's mother came and bent over the child. With gentle hands she felt the fragile body and then broke into loud, mournful cries. Tears poured down her cheeks. In that moment, Olive realized that Aespaneo's grief was genuine. She was weeping over the little girl as if she were her own child.

The next morning Mary Ann whispered her last words to Olive. She called out weakly, "Olive, I am willing to die. I shall be so much better off there." She tried again to sing, but she was unable to do more than whisper the words. Still surrounded by a great crowd of marveling men, women, and children, she lay whispering the words of those beloved hymns, and died.

Although Olive saw the light in her sister's eyes go out, she did not give up. She felt for the child's pulse. There was none. She laid her hand lightly over her face searching for any sign of breathing. Mary Ann was truly gone.

A terrible loneliness filled Olive. She wanted to lie beside her sister and die too. Then she became aware of the bustle on the bluff. Looking up, she saw the Mohaves gathering wood and kindling. They were preparing a funeral pyre for her sister. The chief himself had ordered it.

This was more than Olive could bear. She thought of creeping away and finding some quiet place where she could kill herself. It was then that Aespaneo came to Olive and touched her arm. She said that she knew the white people followed different burial customs, and had begged her husband to let the child be buried in that manner. At last he had given his permission. Tears of gratitude filled Olive's eyes. In a broken voice she thanked the older woman.

The chief came out of his house and told the men to stop building the pyre. He directed two of them to follow Olive's directions in caring for the body. He then handed her three blankets in which to wrap the little girl.

With Olive's help the two men wrapped the body in the blankets. Then, with Olive leading the way, the men carried their light bundle to the plot where the sisters had such joy planting the past autumn. Here, Olive ordered the men to dig a grave about five feet deep. Into this hole they lowered Mary Ann's blanketed body and then started covering it with earth while Olive stood by weeping.

A large crowd of Mohaves had followed to watch. Some of them were weeping with Olive. Others wore serious expressions, as though trying to understand this strange but solemn custom. Many were commenting mockingly about the way the white people treated their dead. After the body was buried, Olive wanted to plant a little wild rose bush on the grave. This, for some reason, they would not allow.

As the crowd dispersed, Olive continued to kneel by the

unmarked grave, weeping and praying for death. She wanted to lie down on the freshly dug earth and die.

At last, faint from hunger and grief, she dragged herself back to the chief's house and lay, sunk in a heavy lethargy. She was roused by Aespaneo's soft voice. The woman was kneeling beside her holding a stone bowl that contained a little corn gruel.

Olive wondered aloud about this unexpected bounty. Aespaneo whispered that she had taken some seeds saved for the spring planting and prepared this gruel. Olive must tell no one, she warned. Angry relatives could kill them both.

Olive accepted the gruel. Later, Aespaneo brought her more. The food helped Olive to revive, but more than the food was lifting her spirits. It was the warmth and concern Aespaneo was showing her, even at the risk of endangering her own life. She could not have been more tender if Olive had been her daughter.

Day by day Aespaneo fed the girl, doling out the food in small quantities so as not to overtax Olive's shrunken stomach. Within three days Olive had regained much of her strength. She began to feel more cheerful than she had in a long while. With her rising spirits came a strange feeling of hope. Olive could not understand why, but she had a new courage and desire to live.

Now she could take care of herself. Remembering her own small store of seed corn, she went to its secret hiding place and took half of it out. She made gruel that she ate sparingly along with an occasional bowl of *oth-to-toa* soup.

With her strength returning and with no need to be back by nightfall, Olive could forage much farther afield. As she collected the roots, she ate what she needed to stay alive before returning to the village and the men's grasping hands. She knew now that she was going to survive.

Chapter Eight

War

Spring brought relief to the whole valley. Birds laid eggs. Sometimes, hunters brought down a few rabbits, though there wasn't much game in the valley. The women were netting fish from the lake, curing them with salt from a nearby salt lick and then laying them out in the sun to dry.

As the spring progressed, the men became more restless. They started speaking of doing battle and winning victories. The inner council of chiefs and subchiefs started holding secret meetings, laying plans for an expedition. Shamans advised them after taking counsel with the wise spirits on the domed mountain.

After performing the rites that, they said, enabled them to contact those spirits, the shamans announced to the council that victory would be theirs. They then picked the auspicious day for the expedition to set out. Runners sped throughout the valley to announce the news. The Mohaves were mounting another expedition against their traditional enemies, the Cocopas, who lived about seven hundred miles away.

Sixty men responded to the call for warriors. The shamans promised victory. A prophecy passed down from generation to generation assured the Mohaves that eventually they would utterly defeat the Cocopas, even wipe them out completely.

The men spent the following days preparing weapons. Bows were tested and restrung; new arrows dipped in a deadly poison made from the juice of a certain plant. Clubs were fashioned from a hardwood tree that grew in the mountains. Stone flakes were chipped into knives with sharp, deadly blades.

While the men got ready for war, the women prepared provisions for them. They did so unhappily because they wanted no part of the coming war. They were vocal about this, using all the arguments they could think of to put a stop to it. The Cocopas had enlisted the aid of powerful allies and would be much stronger than the last time they had fought the Mohaves. This time they might defeat the Mohaves and invade the valley, and there would be wholesale slaughter.

The women's remonstrances had no effect. On the day of departure, a crowd gathered to see the warriors off. The roars of the men mingled with the mournful wailing of the women.

The men rushed off. In that moment a Mohave woman turned to Olive and told her mockingly that if they were in danger, she was in great peril. It was, the woman said, the custom to sacrifice a slave for every warrior slain in battle. Slaves were offered as a gift to the spirits so they would welcome the spirit of the slain warrior when he joined them on the domed mountain. Since Olive was the only captive the Mohaves had, it seemed almost certain that she would lose her life when the men returned.

For some time Olive had been wondering if the Mohaves were bartering with the whites. Occasionally, parties of Mohaves would disappear. When they returned, they would bring with them small articles that could only have come from the settlers. It might be some old battered shirt or dress or a pair of worn-out shoes. That meant Fort Yuma was within reach.

Olive had put off looking for the trail that led to it. Now she felt she simply had to escape. For five months she invented plans but hesitated putting any of them into practice. They all seemed too flimsy to be successful, especially with the disfiguring *ki-e-chook* that marked her like the brand on cattle. Unable to decide what move she should make, she became more terrified. Nights were the worst. Terrible dreams woke her repeatedly.

Then one August day, when Olive was returning from gathering roots, she saw a man running down the slope on the far side of the river. Olive could not make out his tribe at first. When he came closer, she recognized him. He was a Mohave.

Olive watched him descend the hills without slackening his pace. His dogged jogging told her that he was exhausted, so he must have come a long way. Had he traveled from the battle? Was he bringing news of the war? She stood motionless. No one had seen her. There was time to try to escape. She flung herself flat on the ground. She could wait there till nightfall.

She raised her head to watch the Indian disappear into a hut at the outskirts of the village. Then he entered another and then another. From every hut criers began dashing out, rushing through the valley with their announcement. "There is news of the battle! Come to the chief's house and hear it."

Olive looked around her. The silhouettes of the high mountains surrounded her. Doubtless trails led through them, but Olive had no idea where they were or where they went. She hesitated a long while. Then, walking reluctantly, head bowed, she headed for the chief's house, where she waited trembling for the messenger to arrive with his news.

Crowds were gathering in the square. Mohaves looked at

This Mohave man poses among some of the implements of a society based upon agriculture.

Olive with impassive faces. Others grinned at her sarcastically.

Finally, the messenger stepped out of the gathered crowd. "Our warriors have won a great victory!" he cried. "We have taken five captives. None of our people were killed. All are on their way home."

Relief flooded Olive and made her weak. She covered her face with her hands and stumbled away, speaking her thanks to God in a fervent prayer for having again saved her from death.

Within a few days the warriors returned, bringing their captives. For several days the Mohaves celebrated. They shouted and sang and danced until they dropped; feasted on some ripening corn, squash, and pumpkin the women prepared. The women were offered none of the salted fish. It was the custom not to touch salt during the month that a captive was taken.

Olive made friends with the oldest of the new captives. She was in her twenties and told Olive that her name was Nowereha. She was a mother with a ten-month old baby. When she and her husband had been fleeing the Mohaves, he had taken the baby from her so that she could run faster. He had escaped with the child. She was grateful for her husband's action. If her child had stayed with her, he would have been killed.

For a week Nowereha wandered disconsolately about the village. Then early one morning she fled. Soon trackers were on her trail. Olive prayed that the girl would escape and get back to her people. But several days later a Yuma arrived, bringing the captive with him. He had chanced to see Nowereha crouched in the recess formed by an overhanging rock. Recognizing her as a Mohave captive, he had brought her back to them.

The return of the captive triggered a noisy council meeting, followed by a night of wild prancing around the captive.

Dancers shouted insults at the cringing girl and spat in her face. Olive remembered how she and Mary Ann had suffered the same treatment from the Apaches. The Mohaves' behavior this night seemed far more sinister.

"We will soon put you in a place where you can't do any more harm," they shouted.

The next morning, Olive found out what the threat meant. She and the other captives were led to an open space where a cross had been set up. Nowereha hung on the cross. Sharp wooden spikes pierced her hands and feet. Strips of bark, to which thorns were attached, bound her head to the upright post.

"We have brought you here to see what happens to runaway slaves," the Mohaves told their captives. "Watch well!"

With this they began running around Nowereha in circles, stamping, and hurling frenzied taunts at her. Finally, several of them raised their bows and fitted poisoned arrows to them. They began shooting these at the girl. When she cried out in agony, they mocked her with derisive yells.

For two hours Nowereha hung dying while the men shot arrows into her. Her agonized cries rang in Olive's ears. She felt weak and came so close to fainting that the Mohaves had to hold her up. At last, Nowereha died. Her tortured body was taken down and burned on a funeral pyre.

Sickened and faint, Olive listened as the Mohaves warned her and the other captives that Nowereha's fate would be theirs if they tried to escape. From that moment on Olive gave up all hope of trying to leave the secluded valley. She could not banish the memory of Nowereha's tortured face and anguished cries. They would haunt her dreams for a long while.

The men had been gone five months. The wheat Olive and

Mary Ann had planted the autumn before had been growing tall and was beginning to turn golden. Though her squash did not survive, the kernels of corn Olive planted grew tall.

At first blackbirds stole the kernels before they sprouted. Olive could not protect them while she was out grubbing for roots or gathering mesquite seed. Aespaneo drove off the blackbirds, and later guarded the young crops from thieves.

By fall Olive could glean a half bushel of wheat and another of corn. Aespaneo asked the chief to give Olive a safe place to store her crops and make them tabu to all others.

The villagers were also reaping a plentiful harvest, not only of corn and wheat but of squash, pumpkins, and beans. They found that they had more food this year than they had ever had before because of the new land they had put into cultivation.

Time had come for the harvest festivities. Excitement swept the length of the valley as villages prepared for the big event. All of them would be taking part. A village at the north end of the valley was the first to extend an invitation to Espaniola and a few of his people. The invitation came by a crier who announced the time, as well—a moon from that day.

Espaniola's people began their preparations at once. Women started working on the food for the feast—grinding wheat and gathering grass seeds. Pumpkins, squash, beans, corn, everything had to be readied.

The men busied themselves making masks—some out of bark, others out of skin. They were masks of fierce faces, the faces of the mighty spirits who lived on the domed mountain.

On the day set, they gathered at the chief's lodge. Some donned masks; others painted their bodies and faces with black, white, and red patterns or daubed their hair and faces with mud.

Before the party set out, Olive was invited to join the group. The procession moved slowly forward, descending the bluff and marching down the valley. Sometimes they walked in rhythmic unison, at other times in broken, uneven steps, always chanting at the tops of their lungs. As they did so, they waved their arms in wilder and wilder gestures.

About one mile from the settlement of their hosts, they stopped in front of a large mound. Here they built a great fire. As the orange flames swept up into the night, the guests began a wild dance. They circled the fire, singing and dancing until midnight. When the great harvest moon hung overhead, shedding a silvery light over the rustling valley, the dancers dropped where they were and slept.

Early the next morning a procession of women began arriving from the dancers' homes. They came bearing baskets on their heads. The baskets contained dough cakes made of wheat flour mixed with boiled mashed pumpkin. Some cakes were two feet in diameter. The cakes were wrapped in leaves and laid in shallow holes dug in the earth. The holes were covered with sand and fires were lit on top of them to bake the cakes.

Other women brought stone bowls filled with soup or boiled vegetables, or wheat mush mixed with the ground seeds of squash or wild grass. The guests did another dance around the mound. The dance lasted twelve hours, but the hosts did not appear. At the close of the dance, the guests gathered up their food and carried it back to their own homes, where they feasted until the food was gone. Only then did the dancers stop.

This was the first of many such invitations. Sometimes the hosts were in the south end of the valley, sometimes in the north. Sometimes they lived across the river. Espaniola extended several invitations himself. The ceremony was always the same. The guests would dance and sing around the food they had prepared and placed on their hosts' sacred mound. Then without sharing with their hosts, they would take the food back to their own homes to feast on it.

Despite all the feasting, the women had learned a lesson from the famine. They had already prudently stored away enough this year to last well into the spring. As the festivities ended, they went back to planting the fields.

Olive, too, sowed her seed in her small plot. As she worked, a strange sense of peace filled her. It was as though a burden had dropped from her shoulders. Now that she had finally realized that escape was out of the question, she decided to accept her life here. Things were much easier now. She had become used to the monotony of grubbing for roots and gathering mesquite seeds, and was beginning to feel a part of the life of the people. Usually, she was not treated as a slave. Some women had become her intimate friends, confiding their hopes and fears to her.

There were still times when Mary Ann's frail little ghost would suddenly rise to haunt her. These dark periods were becoming fewer and fewer. There were even brief moments when she found herself happy.

That summer, Olive's sense of security suffered when a virulent fever struck. She had seen fevers like this back in Illinois, but this was new to the Mohaves. People were desperately ill. They summoned the shamans to tend them.

The Mohaves divided illnesses into two kinds. One, considered a physical illness, was treated by wrapping the patient in blankets and placing him over boiling water filled with medicinal leaves. Often this treatment sweated out the illness.

Another kind of treatment—a spiritual treatment—was required for malignant illnesses. Then the shaman would go into a trance and communicate with the wise spirits of the mountain. Standing before the patient, he would twist his body into different shapes and wail to summon the healing spirits. When the children of two subchiefs fell ill, the two top shamans worked furiously to cure them. But the children died.

Unfortunately, the shamans had been having little success among their other patients as well. Some of them had died also. Murmurs against the shamans had been spreading. Now the voices of the subchiefs, both powerful men, joined the others. They said the shamans must have made a secret pact with the evil spirits to call down death upon the people of the valley.

The shamans fled to the opposite side of the river. There, with the help of relatives and friends, they managed to conceal themselves for some time. The outcry against them increased as more people fell ill. In the end, to keep peace, Espaniola ordered his men to search out the shamans.

When the shamans were brought back across the river, a mob of Mohaves, mad with grief and terror, assaulted them. The grief crazed mob spat on them, struck them, and called them murderers. Finally, they built a huge pyre and bound the shamans on it. They set it afire, orange flames leaping around the screaming shamans as they burned to death.

Before the summer was over, the epidemic had disappeared. But the memory of what had happened lingered on, destroying Olive's complacency. At any moment, some chance occurrence might rouse the people against her. She could die as had the shamans and the captive Nowereha.

Chapter Nine

Emissary Francisco

Around the end of February, Olive discovered that she was in as much danger as Nowereha and the shamans had been. The day started as any other, with Olive grinding mesquite seeds beside the door of the chief's house. Suddenly, a young boy rushed up to her. He told her breathlessly that a Yuma named Francisco was coming to take her off to the whites.

After the first rush of joy, Olive dismissed the boy's words. It was probably another practical joke being played on her by the idle men who were always looking for a good laugh at her expense. It wasn't long, however, before a subchief came to the house telling the same story. Espaniola sent out criers calling all subchiefs and head men of the villages to a council.

In a few hours, excited crowds began gathering on the bluff. Then the council members arrived and the powwow began. It started with a racket of voices. People shouted at one another angrily, shook their fists, roared accusations and threats.

Olive could not hear what they were saying, but she guessed they were discussing the subject of Francisco's visit. She shivered as her eyes passed from face to face, distorted by the same frenzied anger she had seen before.

In the midst of the noisy confusion, a crier ran in to announce the arrival of Francisco himself. The loud arguments stopped and all eyes turned to stare at the newcomer. He was a well-built man with an air of arrogant authority. Some members greeted him sullenly. Others muttered, "We don't care for the captive." Some shouted loudly that Francisco should be driven away at once. In the midst of the confusion, Olive saw that Espaniola, and the more influential subchiefs, maintained their dignified silence. Then, two Mohaves suddenly hustled her down the bluff and into a village house. They shut her inside and left.

Olive sat alone in the darkened hut. Unprotected by the great chief and his family, she listened fearfully to the yelling that was drifting down from the bluff. It went on all that day and into the night, growing louder and more violent as time went by.

Darkness brought new dangers. Under its cover any member of the mob on the bluff might break away and come stealthily down to kill her.

In her terror, Olive remembered Mary Ann's last words to her, "I don't like to leave you all alone, Olive. But God is with you, and our Heavenly Father will keep and comfort you."

Olive began to pray. She repeated the prayers she had learned in her childhood, so far away now, in so safe a life.

For three days and three nights Olive remained in the hut praying while the racket continued on the bluff above her. From what she had already heard, she guessed that the whites now knew she was here and wanted to rescue her. She felt grateful for their concern but found herself regretting that they had ever heard of her. That knowledge, instead of helping her, might result in her death.

As the third night began to give way to dawn, Olive was released from the hut. She learned that some time during the night the council had closed with a strong refusal to let her go. Francisco left with an order never to return, on threat of death.

Coming out of the hut, Olive realized that, whatever the decision, life would never be the same. The men were now again openly hostile to her. She saw death everywhere in their faces. Some were saying, "The whites have never come to our valley before. Kill her or sell her and they won't come now."

Even the other women who had been Olive's friends avoided her with faces averted. Up on the bluff, Aespaneo's kind face wore a reserved look. Topeka's affectionate gaze was mingled with pity. The chief who held her fate in his hands was no longer a pleasant master, but had become an overbearing tyrant. He curtly ordered Olive to be about her daily work.

Unknown to Olive, Francisco had disobeyed the order to leave at once. Determined to rescue the captive, even if it meant trying to spirit her away some time after dark, he had returned to his camp on the other side of the river, and spent the rest of the night arguing with the subchiefs who lived there. Surely, he pointed out to them, it would be wiser to return the captive than to invite the terrible vengeance the whites threatened.

Francisco was a wily man. Seeing the growing fear in the faces of the subchiefs, he left and began making ostentatious preparations for departure. He was in the midst of this bustle when the subchiefs came to him in a body. They begged him to go back with them to the chief's house and try again to persuade Espaniola and the council to let the captive go. Finally, with a great show of reluctance, Francisco agreed to accompany them to the bluff.

Around noon, the subchiefs and several followers appeared before the chief's house asking for another meeting. At first,

Espaniola refused to let them inside, and several Mohaves threatened to kill Francisco on the spot. But Francisco's large entourage, which included many influential subchiefs, gave Espaniola pause. At last he agreed to hold a secret meeting with some of his advisors, after which he changed his mind.

Once more he sent out the criers to announce there would be yet another council. Meanwhile, several Mohaves went in search of Olive. At first she wondered, terrified, if they had come to kill her. Instead, they told her she was to be part of a plan to deceive Francisco.

They began painting her face, feet, and hands with a dun-colored clay-like substance. After they had finished, they threw a blanket around her that concealed the rest of her body. They told her they were going to introduce her as a member of a race of people much like themselves who lived far away in the direction of the setting sun. They ordered her to talk to Francisco in gibberish and pretend not to understand anything he might say to her in English. If she dared betray them, they would kill her on the spot, and Francisco too. With this last threat, they led her into the council where Francisco was already waiting.

Face to face with him, Olive realized that this was her last and only chance at freedom, perhaps even at life itself. If Francisco were to leave her behind now, she would surely be killed. Conjuring up the language she had not spoken since Mary Ann's death, she began telling him in broken English that the Mohaves were trying to fool him. She was really the American slave he had come for.

At her words, Francisco broke into a towering rage. He jumped to his feet, and in a resonant voice he scolded the Mohaves for their feeble attempt to deceive him and pointed out that the soldiers now knew she was here. They were already arming many soldiers. If he returned empty-handed, or didn't return at all, they would march upon this pleasant valley and destroy it, killing everyone here. Not only that, but they had threatened to kill the Yumas as well. It was out of compassion for his own tribe and for the Mohaves who were the Yuma's allies that he had undertaken this dangerous mission. Now they were repaying his kindness with lies.

The angry crowd broke into shouts and jeers. They became so rowdy that Espaniola had difficulty restoring order. Some wanted to kill Olive on the spot and order Francisco to go back and report her death. Others wanted to kill them both. Some scoffed that the whites were too far away to harm them, so why let Olive go.

No matter how threatening the Mohaves were, Francisco continued to keep a bold, calm front. He answered all their threats with threats of his own, and countered their objections with logical explanations. Finally, as dawn was breaking, he brought out an envelope.

"Take it, take it!" Francisco urged. "Read it!"

With a trembling hand, Olive accepted the envelope, staring at the script that had become so foreign to her after so many years. At last, haltingly, she read aloud the inscription:

FRANCISCO, A YUMA INDIAN, GOING TO THE MOHAVES

Then she opened the envelope and pulled out the letter while the whole council sat in hushed silence, waiting. It took Olive even longer to make out this writing. At last she could decipher the message. It read:

"Francisco, Yuma Indian, bearer of this, goes to the Mohave Nation to obtain a white woman there, named OLIVIA. It is desirable she should come to this post, or send her reasons why she does not wish to come.

MARTIN BURKE,
Lieut. Col., Commanding
Headquarters, Fort Yuma, Cal.,
27th January, 1856"

As Olive studied the message, the Mohaves began clamoring for her to tell them what was there. She remained silent, trying to keep control of her trembling body. She couldn't let them see how anxious she was or let them know how much in that moment she wanted to leave them. Everything depended not only on what she said but on how she said it.

The Mohaves grew more demanding. Men, women, even little children all had crowded into the meeting place. Finally, Olive broke her silence. She began to read the letter aloud. When she came to the end, she continued as though still reading. Following Francisco's lead, she described the large army the whites were gathering, the destruction they were planning to visit on the lovely valley and all its people.

The sun had been up for some time when Olive and Francisco were ordered to leave while the council deliberated again. Shortly afterwards Chief Espaniola called them back. Turning to Francisco, he spoke reluctantly, "It has now been decided. You shall be allowed to take the slave to the whites."

After five years of captivity, Olive was about to be freed. Unable to control her feelings any longer, she burst into a flood of tears.

Chapter Ten

Free At Last

The council's decision to let Olive go brought the Mohaves crowding around her. Some men started laughing sarcastically, exclaiming, "Oh you feel fine now don't you?" They didn't touch her, but their flashing eyes and angry gestures told Olive that given the least chance they would still strike her down. Most of the Mohaves just looked at her with a serious expression, as though they were concerned for her welfare once she had left the chief's protection. Others seemed to be trying to imagine how she would fit into the strange life of the whites now that she had become so like a Mohave herself.

The women who had become her closest friends, among them Topeka and her mother, began openly expressing their joy as they looked into Olive's shining eyes. This was what Topeka had wanted since first seeing the white slaves with the Apaches.

After a breakfast of mesquite mush, the chief and his council met with Francisco to arrange the terms by which Olive was to be released. They told Francisco that the beads and blankets he had brought were not enough, he must provide a good horse as well. Francisco assured Espaniola he could arrange it, and the chief said he would send his daughter along to be sure the bargain was kept.

Meanwhile, Olive and the other women began making preparations for the provisions needed for the long journey. They would consist primarily of mesquite mush, so quantities of the seeds had to be ground. As Olive worked at the familiar task, a strange feeling of homesickness began to overwhelm her. Behind her lay the chief's house, her home for four years. Before her, the beautiful valley wore an emerald sheen from the sprouting wheat; the shining river and brimming lake gleamed like mirrors. The valley looked much the same as when she and Mary Ann had first gazed down upon it. Again, her sister's childish exclamation of joy tugged at her memory, "It seems to me, Olive, I should like to live here."

Even the towering mountains she had viewed as prison walls were now faithful guardians. She knew how they changed with the changing seasons, and even the time of day. This lovely valley where she had grown from childhood into womanhood had become as familiar and dear to her as the distant farm in Illinois. Now she was about to leave it for a life among total strangers—no member of her family left to welcome her.

In the end, Olive paid a visit to the grave of her sister. For the last time she wept over it, thinking of how Mary Ann would have rejoiced at this moment. She longed to take the little body home, although she knew the Mohaves would not allow it. They had already told Olive that when she had gone they would open the grave and burn the body according to their own custom.

There was nothing of Mary Ann that she could take with her except a little string of beads that the child had once worn with such pleasure. Then, as the group was ready to set out, the chief came to her and gravely took away all the beads and the flannel scraps. Olive wept when he took Mary Ann's string, begging him to let her keep that at least. The chief was unmoved. Olive did manage to conceal a few of the small ground nuts. They would be her only mementos of her five years of captivity.

Preparations complete, the small group set off. Francisco was accompanied by a brother and two cousins. One or two Mohave warriors accompanied Topeka. All the men rode horses. Olive and Topeka went on foot. Beyond the green valley, they entered a land sun-scorched and wind-scoured. The trail was as rugged as any Olive had yet traveled. This time she walked it with a light heart.

Topeka told Olive that her father had not wanted to let her go. He suspected Francisco was trying to purchase her for his own people. He had even accused the Yumas of this. The letter Olive read had persuaded the chief.

The little party trudged for eleven days. Sometimes freezing gales whipped up great clouds of sand. They had to cross ice-cold streams running through craggy canyons. Some streams were so swollen with late rains that Topeka and Olive had to swim across them. Topeka skillfully held the roll of blankets she carried high with one hand.

It was during this trek that Francisco told Olive how her release had come about. It wasn't instigated by the army, but by a carpenter who worked at the fort. The Yumas called him Carpentero, although his name was Mr. Grinnell. Francisco said that Carpentero had heard that there were two slaves in Mohave hands and had asked them whether this was true. One night Francisco had come secretly to Carpentero to tell him there had been two slaves but one was now dead. He had then offered to barter with the Mohaves for the other slave, but he would need goods with which to deal.

A carpenter who worked at Fort Yuma instigated the effort to free Olive.

Carpentero had provided these goods out of his own pocket and had persuaded the commander of the fort to write the letter. Francisco told Olive that he had undertaken this venture at great risk to himself, but he was glad to do it for her sake.

Around noon of the eleventh day, three Yuma Indians came running to Carpentero to tell him that they had seen Francisco in the distance accompanied by two young women. Carpentero was ferried across the river to meet the group. He found himself facing the young white woman. Haggard from the long trek, barefoot, dressed only in a short bark skirt, her chin disfigured by the *ki-e-chook*, she shrank back as he presented himself.

It was a time of vindication for Grinnell, who had maneuvered the whole scheme himself. Far from planning to launch an expedition to the valley, Colonel Burke had refused to do more than write the brief, indifferent letter Olive had read.

After Francisco's departure for the Mohaves, Grinnell became the butt of many army jokes. The soldiers had mocked him for thinking that he could purchase anything valuable with a few beads and three blankets. Now they were to hear the word being flashed back to the fort, "The captive girl is here! The captive girl has come!"

Instead of being the fort's fool, Grinnell had become its hero. Excited people were pouring out of the compound to get a look at the travelers who were descending the opposite bank of the river to the ferry landing.

Seeing the soldiers in their smart uniforms and the fully dressed crowds lined up across the river to greet her, Olive became ashamed, aware of her own scant clothing. She drew back, reluctant to board the ferry and appear before all those people as she was.

A guard at the landing realized the reason for her reluctance and sent a messenger back to the fort to explain the situation. Soon the messenger returned with a fine party dress sent by the wife of an officer. There was also an invitation to stay at the officer's home.

Feeling awkward in the unfamiliar bodice and full skirt, Olive stepped aboard the ferry and crossed the river. There she was greeted by a barrage of cheers from the huge crowd, which included both whites and Yumas. As Francisco presented Olive to the fort commander, cannons boomed a salute, making the earth tremble beneath Olive's feet.

Abashed and self-conscious, Olive looked to Topeka for support. Francisco presented the young Mohave woman to the captain, explaining that Topeka's father, Chief Espaniola, had demanded a horse in payment for the captive. Topeka had come to confirm the deal. It must have been with a chagrined smile that the commander quickly agreed, promising the young woman she should have one of the best horses in his stables. Topeka replied gravely that in several days her brother would come to claim it.

All the transactions at an end, Topeka prepared to leave. Olive spoke her last farewell to Topeka. A sudden wrenching sense of loss touched her then. She had come back to her people a total stranger. Her only friend was the young Mohave who had been as close to her as a sister, weeping with her, rejoicing with her, protecting her as best she could. It was she who had persuaded the chief to save the two forlorn sisters from the Apaches. If she had not done so, this rescue would not have been possible. The Apaches, even more implacable in their hatred of whites than the Mohaves, would have killed her before letting her go back to them.

Chapter Eleven

Lorenzo's Story

Everything that had once been familiar to Olive was now strange. She spoke in English mixed with Mohave words.

Olive was stunned at one piece of news. She was not her family's only survivor. Lorenzo had not died from his beating. It had been his efforts to free her that had resulted in her rescue. Ten days later, Lorenzo arrived. For a few minutes brother and sister stared at each other in disbelief. In the five years of their separation they had grown into adulthood. Both had suffered a great deal. But the faces were still familiar. Breaking into tears, brother and sister embraced.

In the days that followed, they described the experiences they had been through. Lorenzo had lain on the bluff, slipping in and out of consciousness. Hearing the screams of his family, he had tried to go to their aid but had been unable to move. He had heard Olive and Mary Ann's sobs as they had been led away.

Lorenzo had been badly injured. He could taste the blood and feel it flowing from his ears and nostrils. He had raised himself on his hands and knees. Falling into unconsciousness again, he had lost his balance and tumbled over the edge of the bluff, landing on a ledge some sixty feet below. When he awakened he said, "I will get up. I will walk."

Lorenzo crept back to the bluff. Again he found himself among the bodies of his family. He could not bear to look at them. Turning his face away, he began crawling along the bluff until he reached the trail. Here, parched with thirst and feverish, he crept into the shade of a large bush and fell asleep.

The sun was setting behind western ranges when he next awakened and started down the bluff, crossed the Gila River, and followed the trail toward the village of Pimole. He walked through the night, taking frequent rests. By daylight he had covered about fifteen miles. Finding himself near a pool of muddy water, he stopped to drink. He didn't mind the rank taste or the feel of grit in his mouth as the tepid water slid down his throat. Immediately afterwards he fell asleep.

Lorenzo slept for a long while and woke up delirious. He had no idea his skull had been fractured, though he could feel the gaping wound on his crown. Hammers pounded inside his head. The pain was so dreadful he was afraid his brain would jump out of his skull. He pressed his hands against either side of his face to keep his brain inside and continued.

The way led across high land. He covered ten miles, but by mid-afternoon he had to stop and sleep. He awakened to howls. A pack of wolves surrounded him. He began yelling and throwing rocks, staggered to his feet and began walking away, hoping to leave the wolves behind. They followed him. Whenever they came too close, he would hurl more rocks and shout at them. All that night and most of the next day he was unable to shake them off. Finally, toward evening, the wolves stopped, turned and loped away, their howls fading in the distance.

Rid of the wolves, Lorenzo lay down and slept till morning. He was so weak with hunger and thirst by this time that in his

delirium he thought of gnawing on his own arms to keep from
starving. Still he struggled on, and by noon came to a dark
canyon where water dripped from the overhead rocks. Here he
assuaged his thirst.

While he was resting, two Pima Indians astride horses came
upon him. Lorenzo recognized one of them as an acquaintance
from Pimole. After hearing what had happened, the Pima
dismounted and embraced the boy. He spread two blankets in
the shade of a tree and made Lorenzo lie down. He handed the
boy a piece of bread and a gourd of water, promising to come
back and take him to Pimole when his errand was done.

Lorenzo slept until twilight, waking to find the Indians had
not yet returned. Feeling unsafe alone here, he set out again,
walking most of the night. By daylight he had become so weak
he could scarcely stagger along. The wound in his head had
become infected, and putrid pus was leaking from it. Parched
and starving, ablaze with fever, Lorenzo lay down under a large
shrub, wanting only to sleep.

After two or three hours, he awakened to see far off in the
valley two moving objects coming toward him. Fearing it might
be hostile Apaches, he crouched under the shrub and stared at
the approaching party. As it came closer he recognized it as two
covered wagons.

Giddy with joy, Lorenzo fainted away. He awakened to find
Robert Wilder bending over him. The Wilders and the Kellys
had decided to cut short their stay at Pimole and continue to Fort
Yuma. Their covered wagons were stopped nearby.

"My God, Lorenzo!" Wilder exclaimed, recognizing the boy
under all the caked blood and dirt. "What has happened?"

Lorenzo sobbed openly as he told them the story of the

massacre. Upon hearing it, the alarmed families decided to return at once to the village. By this time, Lorenzo had been six days on the road. Dehydrated and starving, at times delirious, he was dangerously ill. Only the tender nursing of the Kelly and Wilder women and the Pimas saved him.

Meanwhile, the Wilder and Kelly men gathered a party of two Mexicans and several Pimas and set out for the bluff to bury the Oatman family. When they got there they discovered nothing but bones stripped of all flesh, the work of the efficient desert scavengers—coyotes, wolves, vultures. The men found the skeletons of only seven human beings. That meant Lorenzo was right. Two of his sisters had been taken captive.

A week later six men arrived and agreed to accompany the two covered wagons to Fort Yuma where Lorenzo was turned over to a Dr. Hewitt, who nursed the boy to full recovery. Dr. Hewitt had taken a deep interest in Lorenzo, and when the doctor left for San Francisco he took his patient with him.

It was here that Lorenzo met Dr. Lecount again. The doctor told him indignantly that he had hurried on to Fort Yuma after leaving the family behind. Arriving in a few days, he had informed the commander, Mr. Heinsalman, of the danger the Oatmans were in, and pleaded with him to send a party to escort them to Fort Yuma. If the captain had acted immediately, the family could have been saved.

Instead, the commander had refused at first, despite Lecount's urging. When he finally gave in and sent a couple of men to investigate, it was too late. They had come upon the grizzly massacre and had returned to the fort heartsick and furious, loudly excoriating the commander.

When his benefactor, Dr. Hewitt, had to leave San Francisco

for the East he placed Lorenzo in the care of a local family. That marked the beginning of a terrible time for the boy. Lonely, homeless, and filled with despair, he thought constantly of taking his own life. The only thing that kept him from doing so was the haunting thought of his captive sisters, mistreated, perhaps dying by torture at the hands of the cruel Apaches. Rescuing them if possible began to dominate his every thought.

There was little he could do at the time, penniless as he was. He had to find work of some kind just to keep himself alive. For a while he was employed by the firm of the family with whom he was staying. Then he went to work in the California gold mines. After three years he had enough money to travel to Los Angeles, a favorite stopping off place of emigrants traveling the Santa Fe Trail. He thought that some of them might have news of the Oatman girls and even be willing to help him rescue them.

From among these emigrants, Lorenzo tried repeatedly to recruit volunteers to go in search of his sisters. He would organize a party. A time would be set for departure. But as the hour approached, the men would back out one by one with the excuse that the girls were probably already dead.

When these attempts failed, Lorenzo joined teams of prospectors who were going in search of gold on the Mohave River. Some men promised to turn their trip into a search for the girls instead. They never kept their promises.

Once Lorenzo managed to travel to Fort Yuma and work his way beyond it in a foolhardy search for his sisters. Later he was to learn that he had gone in the wrong direction. In 1855 a new officer, Commander Burke, took charge of Fort Yuma. He assigned five men to join Lorenzo in another search for the

Lorenzo Oatman spent five years trying to win the release of his sisters.

Oatman girls. They spent several weeks scouring Apache territory southwest of Fort Yuma, discovering nothing.

Lorenzo, discouraged and penniless again, returned to California where he found work in a wilderness area. Then one day he received a letter from a friend at Fort Yuma. Mr. Grinnell had information of two white girls held by the Mohaves, who had bought them from the Apaches. They were, he said, members of a family massacred by the Apaches in 1851. Weeping over this letter, Lorenzo immediately wrote a news story for the *Los Angeles Star*. The newspaper had published it, along with an editorial lambasting the army for not going to the girls' rescue. This article and editorial inspired Mr. Grinnell, who had elaborated on the story by adding the threat of United States vengeance should the captives not be freed.

Meanwhile, Lorenzo was not idle. He drew up a petition to the governor of California asking him to send soldiers to rescue his sister. The petition was signed by many people. The governor referred him to the Bureau of Indian Affairs in Washington, D.C. Lorenzo was preparing another petition to send to Washington when a friend showed up one day in the wilderness where Lorenzo was working. Silently, he handed him a copy of the *Star*.

Lorenzo opened the paper and read the headline: AN AMERICAN WOMAN RESCUED FROM THE INDIANS.

The story continued: "A woman giving her name as Miss Olive Oatman has been recently rescued from the Mohaves and is now at Fort Yuma."

Almost five years to the day that the Oatman family had been massacred, Lorenzo set out on horseback for Fort Yuma. He was accompanied by a Mr. Low, who had obtained the horses for himself and the young man. During the long journey of 250 miles, Lorenzo dealt with his doubts. Could it be another captive who had been released? Could the story have garbled the facts? Now, in Olive's presence, he was finding that all the facts were true. Though Mary Ann was dead, Olive, at least, was still alive and standing before him.

Olive and Lorenzo stayed a few weeks at Fort Yuma while Olive settled into the white world again. During their stay, they received another surprise. A cousin whom they hadn't known existed had taken the emigrant trail to Oregon. He had read the news of Olive's rescue and had come to bring brother and sister to his home in the Rogue River Valley.

Accompanied by their cousin, Olive and Lorenzo traveled north to San Francisco where they boarded an Oregon-bound ship. Mary Ann must have been much on Olive's mind during the long trip. Perhaps she was thinking of how the child would have enjoyed this pleasant contrast to the long sunburnt hours they had had to cover on foot.

When Olive finally disembarked on Oregon shores, she remembered a little girl with shining eyes who had once cried out with joy over the green valley of the Mohaves. How she would have loved the sight of this green and fertile land!

Epilogue

Olive and Lorenzo stayed with their cousin in Oregon for a while. There they met a writer named R. B. Stratton who interviewed them and added his own observations and wrote a book. *Captivity of the Oatman Girls* became an instant success and eventually ran through three printings.

Later, brother and sister traveled with Stratton to northern California where they attended school in the Santa Clara Valley, to catch up on their neglected education. By this time, Olive's name was known around the country. People everywhere wanted to hear what she had to say, and Stratton arranged a three-week whirlwind lecture tour for her in the East.

Beginning in New York on March 5, 1858, Olive's lecture tour was a success. She became a relatively well-to-do woman and was able to attend several of New York's prestigious schools.

Things did not go so well for the Mohaves and Francisco, although at first it seemed that good fortune was with them. In a few days, Espaniola's son had arrived to claim his horse. All the officers had come out to welcome him and to express their gratitude to his father for the return of the captive. He left with one of the best horses in the army stables.

Francisco also received praise for having done an act of such great courage. He too was rewarded with a fine horse. His successful negotiations with the Mohaves and the honors he received from the whites added to his stature among the Yumas. They honored him by raising him to chiefdom, showing him the great deference reserved for their leaders.

This good fortune did not last. A year or two after Olive's release, the Mohaves and the Yumas joined forces to wage another war on the Cocopas. This time the Cocopas defeated the Mohaves, slaying some three hundred of them. History does not say whether Espaniola was among those killed.

Whether or not Olive ever heard of this disastrous war and its consequences one thing seems certain. If she had still been with the Mohaves they would have offered her up as a sacrifice for their slain warriors.

Olive's new life was far removed from her experiences as a slave. During her stay in New York, she met a man named John B. Fairchild, whom she later married. The couple moved to Sherman, Texas, where, childless themselves, they adopted a child. From then on until her death in 1903, Olive lived a contented life. But no matter how many years went by, she kept the little jar that contained the ground nuts she had gathered so long ago—a reminder of little Mary Ann and of her life in the valley, and of Topeka and Aespaneo and the kindness they had shown her. It was that kindness that had tempered Olive's earlier harsh assessment of the American Indians. She wrote, "Had it not been for her (Aespaneo), I must have perished. From this circumstance I learned to chide my hasty judgment against ALL the Indian race . . . "

Though life with her husband removed Olive from the

constant scrutiny of the public, she was not forgotten. She became the heroine of many pulp novels. Some of these were romances in which Olive and the chief's son had a love affair. Olive consistently denied all such speculations and rumors, and wrote in her book, ". . . to the honor of these savages let it be said, they never offered the least unchaste abuse to me."

But in 1909, six years after Olive's death, a Mohave began calling himself John Oatman. He claimed to be the child of Olive and the chief's son. Few people if any believed his story, seeing it as just another attempt to capitalize on Olive's name. Still, the little Arizona town of Vivian decided to honor his claim by changing the name to Oatman. Today the town, in its own roundabout way, commemorates the tragic and heroic saga of one of America's pioneer families.

Bibliography

Drago, Harry Sinclair, *Roads to Empire*, Dodd, Mead and Co., New York, 1968.

Driver, Harold E., *Indians of North America*, University of Chicago Press, Chicago, 1969.

Duffus, R.L., *The Santa Fe Trail*, Longmans, Green & Co., London, 1930.

Faulk, Odie B., *Land of Many Frontiers*, Oxford University Press, New York, 1968.

Faulk, Odie B., *Arizona: A Short History*, University of Oklahoma Press, Norman, OK, 1970.

Findley, Rowe, "Along the Santa Fe Trail", *National Geographic Magazine*, Washington, D.C., 1991.

Fireman, Bert M., *Arizona Historic Land*, Alfred A. Knopf, New York, 1982.

Goetzmann, William H., *Army Exploration in the American West, 1803-1863*, University of Nebraska Press, Lincoln, 1959.

Jennings, Jesse D., *Ancient North Americans*, W.H. Freeman & Co., New York, 1983.

Kopper, Philip, *The Smithsonian Book of North American Indians*, Smithsonian Institution, Washington, D.C., 1986.

Marcy, Randolph B., *The Prairie Traveler: The Classic Handbook for America's Pioneers*, Harper Publishers, New York, 1859.

Morgan, Dale, Ed., *Overland in 1846: Diaries and Letters of the California Oregon Trail*, The Talisman Press, Georgetown,.

Powell, Lawrence Clark, *Arizona*, W.W. Norton & Co., New York, 1976.

Readers Digest, Editors, *America's Fascinating Indian Heritage*, Reader's Digest Press, Pleasantville, NY, 1978.

Smith, Robert Benjamin, "Apache Captive's Ordeal", *Wild West Magazine*, Leesburg, VA, 1993.

Stratton, Royal B., *Captivity of the Oatman Girls Among the Apache and Mohave Indians*, University of Nebraska Press, 1983.

Wherry, Joseph H., *Indian Masks & Myths of the West*, Bonanza Books, New York.

Index